HOMOSEXUALITY
in RENAISSANCE
ITALY

VOLUME THREE

(Volume One: HOMOSEXUALITY, The True Lives of the Fabulous Men who preferred Men, The Ancient Greeks; Volume Two: HOMOSEXUALITY, The True Story of Same-Sex Love and Marriage, The Ancient Romans; and Volume Four: HOMOSEXUALITY, Modern Times)

© 2014

Other books by Michael Hone: TROY and Port Beausoleil

Table of Contents

INTRODUCTION

It's been a great pleasure writing this book on Italian male-to-male relations because the Renaissance is the period I prefer. Florence was the place to be, the most beautiful city in Europe, adorned by the most beautiful people God has had the genius to create. There was always something going on, be it the life and scandals of Michelangelo and da Vinci, the plots against the life of the great Lorenzo *il Magnifico*, the hanging of the Pazzi from the tower of the Palazzo della Signoria, the scandals around Lucrezia Borgia and her brother (and some say paramour) Cesare. There was the infamous Pope Alexander VI, their father, who had prostitutes and rent-boys delivered on a nightly basis to the Vatican, and his successor, the Warrior Pope Julius II, himself an ardent boy lover.

In Florence, sexually, things were far less clear-cut than with the Greeks. As I wrote in Book Two, Man/boy love was a given in Greece. It was as serine and accepted and *beautiful* as the blue skies over Hellas. (The Thebans even passed a law proclaiming ''that it is illegal for anyone to maintain that sex between men is *not* beautiful.'') Not so for the Florentines. In fact, Florence seems to have been an intermediary between the Greeks and our civilization today, where New York gays gained a minimum of rights thanks to the Stonewall riots of 1969, and France has just passed a law granting gay marriage (meaning that, legally, I'm now worth any other guy in this wonderful land where I live). So things have thankfully changed since Stonewall, although even now no gay lad would be crazy enough to show his true colors in a school locker room (although I'm sure some do so and what can one say other than, ''You're a better man than I am, Gunga Din!'')

Florence had laws and, most importantly, the spirit of the laws. In the 1300s a lad of just fifteen was castrated and a red-hot poker shoved between his thighs when caught selling his wares; another man was burned at the stake for proclaiming that he couldn't ''see what was wrong in loving a boy.'' But during the 1400s and 1500s, which is the period covered by this book, things had taken a far more pragmatic turn. Death was demanded only when children and young boys (and girls, naturally) were raped or otherwise sexually manhandled. Otherwise everyone was fined, large amounts for men who satisfied their lust on boys, small fines for the boys who rented themselves out. Of capital importance is the fact that everyone in Italy, nearly every man, was doing it to boys, a phenomenon so rampant that the Northerners had a word for it, *florenzen*, and the sodomite was a *Florenzer*.

Modern biographers go out of their way to deny the obvious homoerotic content of a poem or a painting dating from that period. A case in point is Caravaggio's works, one of which, *The Musicians*, shows four young boys, singers and musicians, nearly nude, painted while Caravaggio inhabited the palace of Cardinal Francesco Maria del Monte, a man known for his paternal interest in boys in general and homosexual artists in particular, who introduced homoerotic art into the Vatican, and was known to have been homosexual himself. The palace housed as many as fifty boys, artists like Caravaggio, actors who took part in plays dressed as women when the role demanded it, and castrati, one of whom Caravaggio portrays in his painting *The Lute Player*. Another of his paintings, *The Boy with the Basket*, is of a lad known to be his lover, also semi-nude, also as languorous as the boys in *The Musicians*, his lips sensually parted, his basket filled with fruit known for its sexual symbolism at the time—figs, apples and pomegranates—symbolism so sexually charged that during a priest's discourse, when mentioning fruit before his congregation, he brought on guffaws from the men and snickers from the women (a little like today in Turkey where it is impossible for a woman to order a cucumber because of its other meaning in that language, obliging her to say, "Give me one of those salad things"). Just because a historian wasn't under Caravaggio's bed is no reason to avoid raising his sexual preference, as though we were still living in the times of Savonarola. A man's sexuality is of vital importance because it's the motor, the heart, which motivates a man and makes him function. This is Nature's doing because Nature has dictated that our primal *reason d'être* is the continuation of the species. We can have a say in the matter, we can even buck it, but that would be to the determent of our mental and physical health.

Da Vinci was arrest for sodomy, along with three friends, at age 24. He was held overnight and had to go through a month of hell between two attempts to prove his guilt. As iron proof was not forthcoming, he got off. The penalty was death, but even the few thousands convicted, out of tens of thousands charged, escaped with a fine—a large one for the perpetrator, a small one for the boy if he had given himself freely—and a slap on the wrist. This is what Serge Bramly has to say in his wonderful book *Leonardo*: "Leonardo was not really in much danger from the law. Homosexuality was so widespread in Florence at the time that the legal penalties were never enforced. In spite of the threat of divine punishment imagined by Dante in cantos XV and XVI of the *Inferno*, in spite of repeated fulminations from preachers like Bernardino of Siena, and in spite of an attempt in 1403 to reduce homosexuality by encouraging the opening of brothels. Unable to eradicate it, the authorities were resigned to turning a blind eye to it. There are few examples in Florence in the 1470s of great severity toward homosexuals."

This holds especially true for the Medici who ruled every facet of Florentine life for generations. So where thousands were fined by the Office of the Night, an official organization that kept watch over Florentine mores, the Medici and their numerous friends got off scot free should they inadvertently be discovered in a compromising position. During the life of Lorenzo *Il Magnifico* the Office of the Night arrested 1,700 men for sodomy, as noted by Michael Rocke in his indispensable book *Forbidden Friendships*. As lovemaking most often takes place away from enquiring eyes, one can scarcely imagine the thousands and thousands of pleasure-seeking homoerotic affairs that took place in rooms and under the cover of night, but will be forever anonymous (just like today). Rocke goes on to precise that "In the late fifteenth century, by the time they reached the age of thirty, at least one of every two youths in the city of Florence had been formally implicated in sodomy; by age forty, at least two of every three men had been incriminated." Again, everyone was doing it.

As girls were locked away in Brinks-like security, boys naturally gravitated towards each other, especially as there were no clear-cut rules concerning homosexuality and heterosexuality, and, indeed, the words themselves wouldn't be invented for another 400 years! Since Italian boys were (and are) not only highly sexy in aspect and thoroughly lusty in action, I see no reason why I shouldn't add the Medici, and especially Lorenzo de' Medici, to the list of normal Florentines who lived a normal sexuality, which meant frequent intercourse with both sexes. Andrew Graham-Dixon, in his wonderful *Caravaggio*, takes up where I've left off: "The men of Milan were also known for their singular reluctance to marry. Distrust of matrimony was common enough in sixteenth- and seventeenth-century Italy, especially among the upper classes, to have provoked many comments from visitors. Italian humanists, including Petrarch and Leonbattista Alberti, had railed against marriage as a distraction to the intellect and a potential cause of economic ruin. Nowhere was the misogynistic cult of celibacy stronger than in Lombardy. It did not necessarily entail sexual abstinence, merely a refusal to be yoked to any single woman. The rate of celibacy among the Milanese aristocracy reached unprecedentedly high levels in the second half of the seventeenth century, so much so that it has been calculated that more than fifty per cent of all high-born males in the city never married at all."

It's on the hypothesis that all males were doing it with other males that we'll begin this book with the Medici and the Borgia. Cesare Borgia was accused of sodomizing and then killing the boy many considered as the most beautiful during the Renaissance, Astorre Manfredi, 17, and his brother, age 15, before throwing their bodies, tied together and weighted down, into the Tiber. But before we enter the Florence of the inimitable Lorenzo de' Medici, logic obliges me to give the first honor where the greatest honor is due, to dedicate a few short pages to the greatest artist, the most original mind, the most perfect destiny of all, a man moderate in his life, his tastes and his loves, a man said to have brought joy to all who knew him, and perhaps even preceded Astorre Manfredi in beauty, Leonardo da Vinci.

PART I

DA VINCI
1452-1519

"One can have no smaller or greater mastery than the mastery of oneself." Leonardo da Vinci

Today when we see pictures of da Vinci, it's as an old man. Yet he was once young, and he was gorgeous. Caterina Riario Sforza de' Medici visited him in Milan and found him so much to her taste that she showered him with commands. Caterina was a woman who knew how to appreciate boys, having married three of the most handsome lads in all of Italy, but alas for her, da Vinci was a boy who reserved himself for other boys, most often as gorgeous as he was himself. We'll be meeting Caterina again, by and by, as she played a vital role in Renaissance Italy, and given that she was a woman, her reputation rises to the near superhuman. But allow a small foretaste of this colorful personage. She's in her fortification at Ravaldino that the Orsi want for themselves: "The Orsi, outraged, went back to the palace where they fetched her son Ottaviano, age nine. He was brought back before the walls of Ravaldino and a dagger was placed against the lad's throat, the worst possible nightmare for a mother. The child was obliged to cry out for mercy, alerting Caterina to his presence. She returned to the top of the tower and stared down at the Orsi, their troops and the town people who had desecrated the body of her husband and ransacked her place. She felt she had little to fear as they were all deathly afraid of the consequences of their acts. Spies had already returned to Forlì to inform them that troops from Bologna and Milan were on their way, and they all knew too that the new pope would never accept that even a hair of any of the children be harmed.

"Accordingly, Caterina hollered out the words that have made her famous to this day. She told them all that they could do what they would with her children as she was pregnant again and with *this*, she added, pointing to her loins, she could produce many others. Machiavelli tells us what—or so he wrote—really happened, as was revealed to him by Lorenzo *Il Magnifico*, a friend of Machiavelli. Lorenzo knew Galeotto Manfredi, lord of neighboring Faenza. Galeotto sent a letter to Lorenzo in which he stated that, in fact, Caterina had hiked up her skirt and, pointing to her bare "cunt", wrote Galeotto, had bellowed out her famous words. Galeotto's missive to Lorenzo was to make him nearly as famous as Caterina's repartee." (From Part II of this book.)

Leonardo was gorgeous and so were his boys, beginning with Salaì, magnificent in da Vinci's two paintings, *St. John the Baptist* and *Bacchus*, the absolute ultimate in homoerotic art. The beauty of Leonardo can be admired in Francesco Botticini's *Tobias and the Three Archangels*, Leonardo shown as the first angel; and Verrocchio's *Archangel Michael*.

Salaì was Leonardo's nickname for the boy, meaning Little Devil, bestowed rapidly when Salaì, unmanageable and stubborn, hotheaded and careless, proved to be a liar and a not-so-accomplished--although highly assiduous--thief. This at the prepubescent age of ten. A very close friend of Leonardo's, Giacomo Andrea, was present during one of the first meals shared with Salaì. It is suspected that Leonardo's idea for the Vitruvian Man, the male body made up of two superimposed figures showing four arms and four legs, was originally Andrea's invention, and bares an amazing resemblance to Leonardo himself. Of Salaì Andrea said he was a glutton who ate as much as four monks, spilled the wine and broke whatever his fingers came upon. Another friend, the painter, architect, writer and historian Giorgio Vasari, famous for his book *Lives of the Most Excellent Painters, Sculptors and Architects*, wrote that Salaì was ''a graceful and beautiful boy with curly hair and a delight to Leonardo.'' There is no doubt that he was Leonardo's bedmate, the only question being from what age? Along the line Leonardo drew him with a huge erection, a drawing called *The Incarnate Angel*. But Salaì was such a trickster that he may have drawn in the phallus himself on one of his master's many drawings of him. (Another drawing is entitled *Salaì's Ass*, the boy's buttocks shown surrounded by penises.)

Numerous times Salaì made off with Leonardo's money, but as the painter had endless commissions, he was rich and, at the end of his life, even wealthy. Salaì is said to have bought clothes with most of the lucre he swiped, at one point possessing thirty pairs of shoes. Thirty pairs of shoes and thirty years that the boy would remain by Leonardo's side, at times replaced, as with the handsome Melzi whom I'll present, Melzi to whom Leonardo left half of his fortune, the other half going to Salaì. But most importantly, both boys remained loyal to the master, both present at his side to witness his last breath.

Some find it incomprehensible that Leonardo, known for his exactitude (most sources say it took him 4 years to paint the *Mona Lisa*, others as long as 14), painted *John the Baptist* as an erotic young man and not the usual old prophet in most paintings. The surprise is greater still when we learn that in Leonardo's painting the Baptist was at first totally nude, and that only later were animal skins added (which reminds me of the ''artist'' Daniele who covered up the genitals of Michelangelo's Sistine Chapel men, earning the sobriquet ''the painter of breeches.'') At any rate, Leonardo kept the painting with him to the very end, understandable as *John the Baptist* is the most beautiful portrait of a young man that has ever been put on canvas. He kept the *Mona Lisa* until the very end too, at the Chateau of Clos Lucé, a chateau given to him by François I, who is believed to have held his head as he expired, perhaps his last gaze on Salaì at his bedside or Salaì, much younger, in the painting.

Maybe his last gaze was on the *Mona Lisa*, one might say. But it didn't matter. Both the *Mona Lisa* and the *John the Baptist* had the same enigmatic smile, because *La Giaconda*, too, may have been of Salaì. This is a hypothesis forwarded by some. But perhaps stranger still is the painting called the *Monna Vanna*, a lookalike Mona Lisa right down to the smile, but this one thought to have been painted by the boy Leonardo considered his best pupil, the selfsame Salaì, a self-portrait Salaì did of himself, with breasts. At any rate, at his death the *Mona Lisa* was bequeathed to Salaì and sold to King François I for 4,000 écus. Supposedly a huge number of highly erotic drawings were destroyed at the time by a resident priest, whether under da Vinci's orders or not is unknown.

No one will ever know why the child Salaì was chosen by Leonardo. Leonardo himself said he had come upon him while the child was drawing, and seeing potential, he made enquiries into his family. Finding them poor, he made them an offer they couldn't refuse. Leonardo was thirty-eight, an age when a man begins to think of settling down, tired of running after boys his ever-so-slightly decline in beauty was more and more compensated for by a few easy coins, of which, for him, there was no dearth. Already, at age twenty-four, he'd been arrested by the Florentine Office of the Night, he and a gang of his friends, all accused of sodomy. He got off as the charge was difficult to prove, but it shows that, like other Florentines, he was no parvenu to male-to-male intercourse. His interest for those of his own sex was already well known, as reflected by the male nudes that studded his canvases and notebooks, erotic proof of the mystical attraction men have had for each other since Adam fled the Garden of Eden to a land east of Eden known as Nod, where his sons Cain and Abel inaugurated the eternal spiral of murder. The boy Leonardo and his friends were accused of sodomizing was an apprentice goldsmith, Jacopo Salterelli, age 17, a notorious rent-boy. At that time in Florence there existed special letterboxes that citizens used to denounce other citizens. It was in this way that Leonardo and his companions had come to the attention of the authorities. There were two enquiries, at a month's distance, neither of which turned up enough evidence for a conviction, a conviction that held the death penalty. But as already stated, even if convicted one usually got off with a fine and a slap on the wrist, so common was the event. Serge Bramly in his *Leonardo* concludes: "The authorities were prepared to turn a blind eye to various sexual misdemeanors—homosexuality, incest, bigamy: fairly common forms of behavior, after all—on the condition that public order was not disturbed and that a minimum of discretion was observed." But Leonardo must have suffered nonetheless now that everyone in Florence knew about his indiscretion, including his father.

Leonardo's exposure to boys was literally limitless. In the workshop artists and their models came and went as they discussed artistic issues and gossiped, most of whom were sexually available. And as Leonardo gained in reputation, he was surrounded by a constantly renewed court of extremely beautiful boys and young men, friends and models, many of which adorned his paintings and notebooks, thighs, buttocks and penises from repose to full erection, or, in his words, ''long, thick and heavy'' to ''short, slim and soft.'' He continues: The male member ''has a mind of its own. When we desire to stimulate it, it obstinately refuses, or the opposite. When a man is asleep it is awake, and when he's awake it's asleep. It remains inactive when we want action, and wants action when we forbid it.'' He maintains that ''it'' can at times be dangerous, inundating the world with human beings the world in no way needs, as well as being the entry point for diseases (syphilis having reached Italy in 1495). On one page of his notebook he noted: ''A woman's desire is opposite to that of a man's. She wants the size of his member to be as large as possible, while he wants the opposite, so that neither gets what he's after.'' A friend proudly wrote him about the son the man had just given birth to. Leonardo's response was unexpected to say the least, ''I had once thought you to be a prudent man, but now have proof to the contrary, for you congratulate yourself on bringing forth an enemy whose energies will be directed at gaining his freedom, freedom that will only come with your demise.'' Despite his pessimism Leonardo, both gorgeous and good natured, must have made a lot of boys extremely happy.

The aforementioned Vasari wrote that ''there is something supernatural in the accumulation in one person so much beauty, grace, strength and intelligence as in da Vinci.'' Da Vinci was also said to be preternaturally gentle for the period, kind to rich and poor alike, generous, always in good humor and possessing a sense of humor. Vasari goes on to say, ''Leonardo had such a great presence that one only had to see him for all sadness to vanish.'' As a person he personified what Plato would call the perfect alloy of *virtu*, intelligence and knowledge. Leonardo was born, out-of-wedlock, in 1473 in the Tuscan hill town of Vinci, near the Arno River that flows through Florence. His father was a wealthy legal notary and his mother a peasant. His full name was Lionardo di ser Piero da Vince, meaning Leonardo son of Messer Piero from Vinci. He lived his first five years with his mother, then with his father who married four times, but never Leonardo's mother. He was a bastard but that had few ill effects in Renaissance Florence. Caterina Riario Sforza de' Medici whom we met above was also a bastard. Yet she received an education equal to that of boys. On the other hand, bastards could not hold certain positions. They couldn't be notaries, the position of his father which would certainly have become his own had he been born in wedlock—to the loss of the entire world. He couldn't become a doctor, either, a pursuit he might well have chosen, given his love of science. In the case of bastards only the father's name was registered, the opposite of today. Leonardo was an extremely private person all of his life, and only wrote of two incidents that marked him, the first a kite that swooped down over his cradle, the tail of which caressed his face, the second was discovering a cave while exploring the mountains, and although fearful of the monsters it might contain, he nonetheless overcame his fear by venturing inside. A little later he painted the monster he'd imagined on a shield, the perfection of which pushed his father to sell it to an art dealer who in turn sold it to one of the most redoubtable lords of the time, Galeazzo Maria Sforze of Milan, whom we'll meet in Part II of this book.

At age fourteen he was apprenticed to the painter Andrea di Cione, known to the world as Verrocchio, in whose *Archangel Michel* we see the incredibly beautiful Leonardo. The choice of Verrocchio was fortuitous as his paintings are exquisite, the demonstration that Fortune never ever stopped looking over Leonardo's shoulder. Verrocchio's shop was in Florence, another lucky break as it was then, as today, arguably the most beautiful city in the world. Verrocchio never married, but this was true of half of the male population of Florence for whom freedom to live their lives as they wished was of prime importance. Happily for them, they hadn't lived in the times of the great Augustus who obliged the nobility to marry before the age of thirty so that Rome would have the men it needed to run the city, farm the land, and enforce its army. But when a Florentine did marry, it was around the same age as in ancient Rome, thirty. Verrocchio's apprentices included Ghirlandaio, Botticelli and Botticini, whose *Tobias and the Three Archangels* features da Vinci. At age twenty Leonardo's father set him up with his own workshop, but his love for Verrocchio was such that they worked together until Verrocchio's death. Verrocchio was a father figure, perhaps the most important man in the artist's life.

Verrocchio was described by Serge Bramly in his marvelous *Leonardo* as ''a sort of one-man university of the arts.'' He knew and taught literally everything with the exception of huge wall murals, the reason for the disastrous destruction of the *Last Supper*, discussed herein later. When Verrocchio was only 17 he had struck a boy, age 14, with a stone, killing him. He was jailed but released when it was proven that the incident had been an accident. Verrocchio was nonetheless haunted by what he had done to the very end, especially as he was a good man, sensitive in the extreme. Verrocchio's father died the year of the accident and Verrocchio found himself at the head of a family consisting of his mother and six brothers and sisters. Years and years later, now well-off, he was still providing for them as well as his nephews and nieces. Verrocchio was apprenticed to a goldsmith and began learning the skills of drawing, engraving, carving and metallurgy, followed by other jobs in which he would master sculpturing, painting, the basis of architecture and his favorite subject, mathematics. He was commissioned to make the tombstone for the person who started the Italian Renaissance, Cosimo de' Medici whom I'll discuss at great length in Part II. Verrocchio establish his own workshop, a large room with all the instruments an artist uses on the surrounding walls, plus sculptors' turntables, workbenches, easels and kiln, as well as shelves bent by the weight of busts and plaster body parts. The production of the workshop was phenomenal as it touched numerous aspects of daily life. Verrocchio and his apprentices turned out banners, coats of arms, caparisons for horses, designs for embroiderers and weavers, pieces of armor, candelabras, bells and furniture, as well as decorating wooden chests and painting canvas for tents. Whatever could be artistically created or ornamented was undertaken by Verrocchio. Around the workshop and upstairs were the living quarters for the boys and the kitchen.

An apprenticeship lasted around thirteen years, which started with sweeping the workshop and cleaning the materials, moved to the rudiments of drawing, making paintbrushes, preparing canvases and pigments freshly ground every day; sculpting, painting, drawing, decorating; even learning how to make salts out of human excrement—from dawn to dusk, seven days a week. One of the most incredible contracts given to Verrocchio was the placement of a round ball with cross on the very top of the dome of the cathedral Santa Maria del Fiore. In pictures it looks tiny, but it measured six meters across and weighed over two tons. Placed on the dome built by Brunelleschi, the widest to exist at the time, without buttresses or external supports, the dome was considered a miracle, the completion of which Brunelleschi kept secret. A modern understanding of how he did it, based on physical laws calculating stresses, finally ended the enigma, but at the time Brunelleschi had relied on intuition and large-scale models. In all, the dome took 37,000 tons of material, including 4 million bricks. This was in 1469. In 1600 the ball was struck by lightening and destroyed (but later replaced by a still bigger one). After this came commissions for the tombs of Giovanni and Piero de' Medici (the Medici will be fully discussed in Part II), bronze tombs like jewelry boxes with foliage and garlands. The workshop was literally overwhelmed by orders from the Medici, for their palaces, villas and celebrations.

The workshop became the artistic center of Florence where one exchanged ideas, models, recipes for paint and varnishes, where philosophy was disputed and gossip swapped. Of special interest was the new Flemish technique for mixing paint with oil instead of water, making for brighter and more long-lasting colors and smoother gradations of tints. Songs were sung and music was played, as Verrocchio was an accomplished musician. He was truly a kind of Pericles who created the conditions for geniuses to thrive—much of which was perhaps due to his attempt to compensate for having killed a lad of 14.

Like all boys, Leonardo liked to dress up and nowhere in world history was there a better, more exciting city than Florence under the Medici. The costumes for festivals and carnivals (designed by Verrocchio and company) were magnificent. Boys' trousers so tight they looked painted on, ample shirts that fell from the collar bones to the upper thighs, taken in by a thin belt at the waist, shirts that scarcely covered the cloth over the genitals, held in place by two ribbons. A headband with perhaps a feather adorned the forehead. This is how I described Juan Borgia in Part II: "As virile as his father, slim waisted and certain of his sex appeal, Juan swaggered through the streets of Rome in what can only be described as gorgeous attire, a cloak of gold brocade, jewel-encrusted waistcoats and silk shirts, skin-tight trousers with drop fronts--cloth attached by ribbons that would free a man's loins when he wished to piss or perform other virile activities." As Niccolò Machiavelli said, "The city's youth, being independent, spent excessive sums on clothing, feasting and debauchery. Living in idleness, it consumed its time and money on gaming and women." And boys, as we'll soon see.

At age twenty-four, as mentioned, Leonardo was arrested for sodomy. Four years later he moved in with the Medici, with Lorenzo *Il Magnifico*, thanks to whom commissions began to rain down on the boy. From there he went on to the career for which he is known the world over. Salaì followed in his footsteps, helping with his paintings, constructing the machines inspired by the master, keeping shop for the man who would reward him with a golden retirement, providing Salaì with a piece of land and the money on which to build a home. Salaì would later die in a duel, some say by sword, others by firearms, still others by a crossbow.

Salaì was the gift of God that those of my sexual persuasion could rightly give thanks for each and every day left to us on earth. A saner man than Leonardo would have thrown him out when the boy stole his first lire, or when caught in bed with another of the master's apprentices. But the genius whom we are all acquainted with, the master of every domain that took his interest, revered the boy as his source of inspiration, as the cherished love of his life. Leonardo could see beyond the daily tribulations and petty treasons. Instead, he held firm to the companion with whom he would walk the rocky path of life, right up to the end. That Salaì was beautiful and beautifully built was important, without doubt, but in a land like Italy, with apprentices he had to turn away in droves, he could have found a dozen replacements. But Leonardo knew that in the end one goes ahead alone or one grants the concessions necessary to share the route with another. The alternative is sterile old age, the shipwreck so well described by de Gaulle in his *Memoirs*.

One of the most impressive realities concerning Leonardo's notebooks is that amidst the thousands of pages there is nearly nothing of a personal nature about the master himself. We have his thoughts, observations, calculations, recipes for mixing oils and ground paint, machines of all nature, fortification, anatomical drawings, male genitalia galore, all in reverse left-hand writing, much of which is illegible.

The second love of Leonardo's life was Giovanni Francesco Melzi who became his apprentice around 1508. The boy's father was a senator and a captain in Louis XII's army. (More about Louis XII and his invasion of Italy in Part II.) Unlike Salaì who only partially succeeded as a painter, Giovanni Melzi did some remarkable works. As handsome as Leonardo had been in his youth, Giovanni followed his master to the end, inheriting half of his oeuvre. The Melzi family property was at Vaprio d'Adda, an enormous mansion, nearly a small Versailles, witness to the Melzi wealth. It was he who informed Leonardo's family of his master's death. Then he returned to Vaprio d'Adda with his master's notebooks and several paintings. He wrote a book drawn from Leonardo's observations about painting, which eventually found its way into the Vatican. The historian Vasari contacted Giovanni for help with the book he himself was writing. About Melzi Vasari wrote, ''Sir Francesco Melzi, a Milanese gentleman, entered da Vinci's service as a young and extremely good-looking adolescent. He was very dear to his master and today is a noble and handsome old man.'' Giovanni left a son, Orazio, who sold off the notebooks bit by bit. His self-portrait, proof of Giovanni Milzi's wondrous beauty, can be found near my own home, at the Musée Bonnat, Bayonne France.

They met when the boy was 15 and Bramly writes that they took to each other immediately. The questions I have on the couple are those expressed by Bramly whom I would much prefer to take over here: ''He addresses his young friend as 'Messer Francesco' on account of his noble rank, but immediately after this polite formula, we read: 'Why in God's name have you not replied to any of the letters I sent you? Just wait till I get back, and by God I will make you write till you are almost sick of it.' By now Salaì must have been twenty-seven or twenty-eight. One wonders how he viewed his master's friendship with this wealthy, presentable, and highborn youth—as different from himself as day from night. It cannot have been easy for him. Harder to understand are the reactions of the Melzi family. Young Francesco soon announced that he wished to follow da Vinci as a pupil, to be initiated into the art of painting. How would his parents take it? It was quite unprecedented for the son of a good Lombard family to soil his hands with paint. Francesco Melzi was never to leave Leonardo's side, nursing him when he was ill, handling studio affairs, taking all sorts of notes from his dictation.''

Leonardo went to Milan where he was happy to put himself under the patronage of Ludovico Sforze (again, much more in Part II) who paid him extremely well and allowed him all the time he wanted in order to do exactly what Leonardo himself wished to do, and this for 18 years. Then Louis XII invaded Italy (Part II) and Ludovico lost it all, eventually imprisoned by the French king until his death. Leonardo returned to Florence, age 48. The Medici had been expulsed and the Republic reestablished. Savonarola had gone up in smoke and a new breed of artist had arisen, led by Michelangelo and later by Raphael. His father was still there, age 74, with his forth wife and eleven children still at home, aged 2 to 24. Leonardo had written him often, always beginning with ''Dearly beloved father...'' a tender loving son, even if the reality of their closeness was perhaps other. At age 50 he hooked up with Cesare Borgia who appointed him military engineer, a position Bramly says he deeply desired. Cesare was a bastard as was Leonardo, and Bramly goes on to say: ''these two bastard children, having created their own lives, respected each other for their intelligence, independence of mind, and scorn for convention. Leonardo must also surely have been susceptible to Cesare's boisterous elegance and superb bearing.'' All certainly true as Cesare was virility personified. But unlike Leonardo, Cesare, age 27, was the adored son of his father, Alexander VI, who would continue to love him even after Cesare murdered his brother, Juan--the son Alexander cherished even above Cesare. To have the backing and limitless wealth of his father, the pope, was a huge morale booster. Cesare went on a conquering spree and Machiavelli accompanied him. About Machiavelli's *Prince* Jean Giono wrote: ''It is the most objective study of mankind to date, the study of passions treated dispassionately, as if solving a mathematical problem.'' With the death of Cesare (to be fully covered) Leonardo returned to Florence where the town leaders, reigning from the Palazzo Vecchio, wanted him to paint a huge wall in the Palazzo itself. He covered the wall with an immense sketch of the *Battle of Anghiari* (won by Florence against Milan). On another huge wall in the same room Michelangelo, age 29, was commissioned to do the *Battle of Cascina* (won by Florence over Pisa). Leonardo worked on the sketch and preparations for the painting for three long years. After a first attempt failed due to the preparation of oils (apparently a huge problem before the oils were prepared by stabilized manufacturing), he simply returned to Milan under the auspices of Louis XII who was such an important ally to Florence that the leaders had to bite the bullet over Leonardo's departure. Michelangelo never finished his painting either. Called to the Vatican by the war pope Julius II, he would spend four inhumanly difficult years on the Sistine Chapel. Da Vinci's sketch of the battle was treated as a national monument until the return of the Medici, who had it painted over (by none other than the great art historian—but also painter—Vasari!).

Both Michelangelo and da Vinci had only their love of men in common. The painted nudes of Michelangelo were peaches-and-cream clean, those of da Vinci homoerotic wet dreams (although Michelangelo's statues were, homoerotically speaking, to die for). The first, da Vinci, had been handsome, the second, Michelangelo, never. The first was now old, the second just starting out on the road to eternal glory. Bramly recounts the story of Leonardo sitting at a café talking about Dante. He was asked a question, but seeing Michelangelo who was walking past said something like, ''Ask Michelangelo.'' The great artist, always on the offensive, perhaps due to his looks and uncouth appearance, answered, ''Explain it yourself, you who made a model of a horse you could never cast in bronze and which you gave up, to your shame.'' Which was true, but the clay model of the biggest horse ever made—with the exception of the Trojan Horse—was destroyed by the French army when they entered Milan in 1499 and, anyway, Ludovico Sforza had used up the bronze to make cannons. But *500 years later* an American pilot, Charles Dent, had the horse built, thanks to Leonardo's sketches, and offered it to Milan where it now stands! Bramly's story shows that things were not always peachy between the two men, but with Michelangelo personal relationships rarely were. For that, he had to fall in love, which we'll see, in detail, much later. When in love Michelangelo gave himself body and soul; da Vinci was perhaps too cerebral to do so completely.

Vasari tells us that it was around this time that a boy, 20, living in Urbino, decided to forget everything he had ever learned about art and dedicate himself to copying Leonardo's paintings, paintings that had just come to his attention. The boy had a magnificent name, Raphael.

In Milan the French reserved a wonderful reception for Leonardo who, for Louis XII, was the reincarnation of the Renaissance itself. He started the Mona Lisa but the history of the painting is far to complicated to be approached here. It's the Churchillian riddle wrapped in a mystery inside an enigma. We're not sure even who ordered it, let alone who sat for it, although many think it was Salaì himself. (Michelangelo always had men pose for his statues of woman, as well as some portraits.)

While battles for an against Louis XII whirled around him, Leonardo was creating another work whose importance would span a period of 400 years: it was a study of the human body, dissected with perfection and drawn with a detail that takes one's breath away. In his own words (and 200 illustrations) he tells of accompanying an old man in his last hours, how the man complained of no physical pain, only weakness, and how he gently slipped from life into death. To find out the cause Leonardo did an autopsy, discovering that the artery supply to the heart and lower members had withered, describing, for the first time in the history of medicine, arteriosclerosis. Bramly takes over: "One wonders what it felt like to plunge a knife into the thorax of an old man one had been speaking to not long before." Later in his notes Leonardo describes examining a hanged man, his penis engorged, of which he made detailed drawings. Leonardo went on to say that even if one had a love for dissecting, one's stomach might find it disgusting, and one might "be afraid to stay up at night in the company of corpses cut to pieces and lacerated and horrible to behold."

Politically, there was movement. Ludovico Sforza's son Maximilian Sforze recovered Milan, expulsing the French back across the Alps. Pope Julius II died and was replaced by Leo X, the youngest son of Lorenzo *Il Magnifico,* enabling the Medici to reconquer Florence after twenty years of disgrace, and bring an end to the Republic. Leo X was destined to die of gout, as did the majority of the Medici, so rich they could afford the richest food (the cause of gout), but Leo X surpassed them all in girth. He had nonetheless brought a cultural revolution to Rome and was flattered by his followers as he who introduced the reign of Apollo, an esthetic age of gold. Leo X's brother, Giuliano de' Medici, one of many patrons of art supposed to have commissioned the *Mona Lisa,* convinced Leonardo to come to the Eternal City where the artist found himself eclipsed by the new stars of the Renaissance, Michelangelo, Titian and Raphael, Raphael who was paid 12,000 ducats for his works, while da Vinci was offered a measly 33 ducats a month, bringing the quip to Leonardo's mouth, "The Medici created me and destroyed me." He was now old, but his greatest triumphs, his *St. John the Baptist* and his *Mona Lisa* were still to come. He spent three unhappy years in the service of Giuliano, part of which was dedicated to building canals that would drain fever-breeding swamps from around Rome—aided by the intelligent Melzi. The works he initiated were completed 300 years later.

Finally came his encounter with the man with whom he would end his life, François I, age 19, a giant at 6 feet, who loved war, placing himself in the front lines, and was an insatiable womanizer. He recaptured Milan and Ludovico's son Maximilian Sforze, but instead of throwing him into a dungeon he welcomed the lad to his court and pensioned him off. Leonardo made the trip to the Loire Valley, but only after the death of Giuliano de' Medici. The year was 1516; da Vinci had 3 years left to him. He became François' tutor, and their days and nights were filled with discussion, often in the presence of Salaì and Melzi, all three immeasurable comforts to the old man, old beyond his years as we see in his self-portrait.

The last words will be Melzi's, in a letter he sent to Leonardo's surviving brothers: "He was the best of fathers to me and the grief I feel at his death is impossible to express. As long as I have breath I shall feel an eternal sadness, for every day he gave me proof of a passionate and ardent affection. Each of us will mourn the loss of a man such that nature is powerless to create another.''

VASARI
1511-1574

Giorgio Vasari is a hallowed name in art history, as is Plutarch in political science. Born in Tuscany, he started his artistic life as an apprentice in stained glass and then moved to Florence where he was immersed in humanism, an education which is clearly visible in his marvelous work, *Lives of the Most Excellent Painters, Sculptors and Architects*. He was the first to use the word Renaissance in print. He lived in Rome and Naples, learning and painting as he went from confirmed artist to professional in frescoes. Known for his architecture, it was he who built the corridor that connects the Palazzo Pitti to the Uffizi, built under the order of the Medici who wished to pass from one to the other without being seen, as well as frustrating attempts to assassinate them. He loved to fill his book with anecdotes like the boy Giotto painting a fly on a painting by Cimabue that the master kept trying to brush away. His book, paintings and architectural constructions made him wealthy, allowing him to retire to his hometown of Arezzo where he built himself a palazzo that is now a museum. For obscure reasons Vasari turned against Cellini, even though, as Cellini writes in his autobiography, he had provided Vasari with boys on numerous occasions, one of which Vasari badly scratched while in the throes of orgasm.

PART II

COSIMO – FRANCESCO SFORZE – FRA' FILIPPO LIPPI – LORENZO *IL MAGNIFICO* – FEDERICO DA MONTEFELTRO – THE BORGIA – THE SFORZA – CATERINA RIARIO SFORZA DE' MEDICI – ASTORRE MANFREDI

Man is stirred physically, mentally and, of course, sexually. Whether we like it or not, sex is the motor that rules the world, now as then. Cesare Borgia wanted armed power and sexual conquest, an easy equation for him as he possessed military genius and physical beauty; another condottiero whom we'll soon meet, Federico da Montefeltro, had lost an eye in battle and compensated by having his nose surgically hollowed out so he could see in all directions with but one eye. His might and wealth assured him a warming presence for his bed.

Sexual satisfaction was by far the norm in the man's world of the Renaissance, but not exclusively. Caterina Sforza, of Imola and Forlì, used her position as regent to put her stable boy into her bed, an extraordinarily handsome lad murdered by her subjects who found him wanting in class, only to be replaced by another even more handsome suitor. But as might made right then as today, she was conquered by Cesare Borgia who wanted her lands. He raped her multiple times before turning her over to his tavern companions. Lucrezia Borgia was another free spirit who would know more love and the loss of love, debauchery and suffering, than mere mortals like myself would know in several lifetimes.

Throughout the book I'll approach Renaissance sexuality more completely, but for now I'll limit myself to the intellectual and militaristic impulses of the times, and what better place to begin than with one of the bright lights of the period, the Florentine Cosimo de' Medici, father of the future Lorenzo *Il Magnifico,* the star of the Renaissance.

The story of Cosimo begins to the north of Florence, in the city-state of Milan, ruled by Duke Philippo Maria Visconti, a hugely ugly and hugely fat recluse who kept to his fortress away from the sight of those--ambassadors, kings, emperors and the like--who might judge his physical hideousness. He had a dream, that of becoming lord over as much of the land surrounding Milan as militarily possible, a dream that led him to attack the Romagne, home of tiny fiefdoms such as Forlì, Imola and Faenza. He also attacked the Florence of Cosimo de' Medici. But before the attack, let's picture this incredible excuse for a human being. He was paranoiac to the extreme, switching bedrooms as many as three times a night to avoid assassination. He murdered his older brother Gian Maria, a ruler of incredible cruelty who dressed his dogs to devour whomever he sicced them on. During one of the wars Gian Maria waged, the people of Milan, starving to death, pleaded with him to decree peace. In response he had his soldiers massacre 200 of them. From then on he forbade the word "peace" in Milan, under pain of death. When he found his wife lacking in enthusiasm to be covered by his walruse-like blubber, he accused her of having an affair with a young page and had her beheaded. He then married a girl whom he expulsed from the palace when, on the wedding night, the superstitious duke heard a dog barking—naturally, an evil omen. Before taking any decision he had his astrologers indicate the place and time for each of his actions. But he did have time to father an illegitimate daughter, Bianca.

The attack of Duke Philippo on Florence pushed Cosimo to hire a mercenary, the extraordinary Francesco Sforza. Cosimo wanted Francesco to destroy the power of Milan but Francesco Sforza hesitated before entering the city-state as he had plans to marry Bianca and take over Milan without having to wage war. His plan worked, he married the beauty, but as Duke Philippo had not formally named him as his successor, Milan declared itself a republic on Duke Philippo's death, a mere hiccup for Sforza who garrisoned the town and had himself declared duke. But

Sforza's contacts with Cosomo had been so humane and intellectually stimulating that Milan and Florence became friends. Cosimo backed Sforza financially to such an extent that Cosimo's palace became, literally, the Bank of Milan.

Venice, ever afraid of the hegemony of Milan, decided to send troops against both Florence and Milan. Florence appealed to Charles VII of France, a super power that made Venice withdraw simply by threatening to intervene. To thank Charles, Florence acknowledged France's age-old claim to Naples. Furious, Naples decided to go to war with Florence and sent troops to capture the city. Venice too decided to intervene again. Cosimo became literally sick due to the new circumstances and took to his bed. Then two miracles occurred. Naples had to withdraw its troops from the outskirts of Florence when France sent troops to make good its claim on Naples, and Venice had too withdraw its troops when Constantinople fell to the Turks, the greatest threat ever to Venetian trade. For added safety, Venice united with Florence and Milan and an era of peace descended over the former belligerents. To make doubly certain that peace would last, Cosimo sent the most precious of his possessions, a manuscript by Livy, to Ferrante, King of Naples—itself now safe thanks to the timely death of Charles VII. Ferrante was a humanist who loved ancient learning, as did Cosimo himself. Overjoyed, Ferrante promised eternal peace between Naples and Florence.

So here we have the powers that will concern this story as it unfolds: Milan, Florence, France and Naples—we can't count Venice because the Serenissima was too busy making money to really care what was going on outside its waters. Papal authority will remain inefficacious until the advent of Alexander VI, followed by Jules II. Then all hell will break out.

I began Part II referring to war and carnage. But Italy was far from the only country where we find the inhumanity of men. At the exact same moment, to the East, another despot reigned. Vlad the Impaler was known by his father's name, Dracul, meaning son of the dragon. His father ruled Wallachia. He was a warrior who dedicated himself to the protection of Christians against the hoards of Ottomans of whom he is credited with impaling tens of thousands. As a boy he spoke Romanian and learned Greek, German and Latin, combat skills as well as geography, mathematics and science. Vlad and a younger brother, Radu the Handsome, were sent by their father to the Ottomans as hostages and there Radu converted to Islam. The Ottomans taught the boys warfare and horsemanship. Vlad's father was overthrown and Vlad's older brother, who should have succeeded his father, was blinded and buried alive. When Vlad eventually came to power in Wallachia he strove to increase both the defenses of the country and his own political power. He had the nobles he held responsible for his father and brother's murders impaled. When Turks arrived to reclaim tribute from Wallachia he requested that they remove their turbans in respect for his person. When they refused, he had the turbans nailed to their heads, killing them all. The Turks sent an army that Vlad defeated; the soldiers were impaled with the highest stake reserved for their general. The pope and the Venetians--whose trade had been disrupted by the Turks--were wild with joy at the news. But Vlad's little brother who had converted to Islam, Radu the Handsome, came at the head of Janissary battalions to destroy his Christian brother. In addition, he promised that the nobles in Wallachia who had lost their positions because of Vlad would recuperate their entire wealth. Vlad was thereafter assassinated under unclear conditions and beheaded. His reputation for evil spread through Germany and Russia. How much is true will never be known. He was said to have children roasted and then fed to their mothers, and to have the breasts of women cut off and forcibly fed to their husbands, before impaling them all. It is also reported that the Ottoman army turned back from the Danube, in horror, when they came across thousands of rotting corpses, all impaled.

After the fall of Rome the lights went out over Europe. New Christians like Charlemagne were proud of their ignorance, declaring that they were above grammar. Charlemagne gave a choice to conquered peoples, either they convert or they would fall to the sword. During just one morning 4,500 were beheaded when they hesitated. In Constantinople the first emperor to convert, Constantine, watched helpless while 3,000 Christians died under the sword of other Christians over the interpretation of the new faith, and during the Fourth Crusade the city itself was sacked and the inhabitants massacred when the crusaders failed to receive the monies the new emperor promised them. Saint Augustine, after a youth of depravity, declared that a child was already polluted in the womb, as he had been conceived through lust. People converted easily thanks to the promise of the afterlife, but went on with everyday violence in which thousands died in drinking brawls, sexual disputes and sports such as tournaments. Fear of disease and plague, invasion and famine, lightening and floods, dark forests of boars, bears and wolves, all combined to unite families in backward villages, where incest and a limited gene pool assured mental deficiency. Hunched over, afraid of every storm, medieval men lived out their existence is pure anonymity. There were no clocks, not even calendars among them, and even the century in which they lived was both unknown and of no importance. The Great Schism—a pope in Rome and one in Avignon—was unknown to the peasants who passed their days in perpetual toil, seeking out the church at the time of baptisms, marriages and deaths, alongside priests as ignorant as they. Illiterate, pockmarked, gullible, superstitious, for them there were no changes anywhere simply because they were unaware of all. They didn't even have surnames, because none were needed. Only later, when the ancient world was rediscovered, did the individual begin to emerge from the formless masses. Then they would take names in order to distinguish one from the other—the smithy became Smith, the tailor Taylor. Anonymity: nothing is known of the twenty-three generations it took to build the cathedral of Canterbury. But finally names emerged from the mist, those of da Vinci, Michelangelo, Botticelli, all thanks to the rediscovery of the ancient texts, a rediscovery and a rebirth: a Renaissance

The serpentine road from the Middle Ages through the Renaissance and on to Modern Times took centuries to unfold. It was this reemergence of the past, it was the heritage of a very distant Rome and Greece. It was the freedom of the human mind, a mind that turned to individual thought and rationalism over crass religious doctrine and its foundation--faith. Humanism is thought to be anti-religion, but at the time the humanists were believers in religion who simply wanted to reform certain religious practices. Those who no longer believed in religions, and there were certainly few, were heretics and candidates for the stake—a real-life burning bush, a strong incentive not to wander too far from the beaten track. The belief in the separation of the church and state, and the right not to believe in certain dogmas at all, would come—albeit only partially—near the 1700s, with Voltaire.

Petrarch is not only the founder of humanism, but also the very inventor of the term Middle Ages. His endeavor was to free Middle-Ages man by bringing back such thinkers as the Roman Cicero (slaughtered at the hands of Marc Antony who wished to still Cicero's truths). Along with the great Boccaccio (immensely readable to this very day), he also freed access to ancient works by reproducing them in the vernacular, Italian.

The Florence of Lorenzo *Il Magnifico*'s grandfather, Cosimo de' Medici, helped found humanism with his friend Niccolò Niccoli. A banker, Cosimo offered Niccoli the funds necessary to send him far and wide, even to the Holy Land, in search of the ancient manuscripts that would bring the words of the likes of Plato into the very living rooms and libraries of the Medici, hundreds and hundreds of volumes. Each discovery that Cosimo made, each old text he unearthed, was like Howard Carter peering into the tomb of Tutankhamen. Cosimo employed forty-five copyists to spread the liberating concepts of the ancients, assisted by Niccoli who wore a Roman toga to the embarrassment of his entourage. Greek studies became a part of Florentine university instruction and artists like Donatello and Brunelleschi built their art along classical lines. The distinction between Platonic truth and beauty and Plato's ideal republic diverged sharply with Cosimo's continued religious beliefs, among them that he was committing a mortal sin by applying, as a banker, usury to his loans. And then, each time civilization advances a step, it seemed (and seems) that something came (comes) along to set it back, forcing men on their knees before some god or other, because of man's lack of faith in himself: wars, disease, the horrors of the Black Death, civil strife, illness, sent men back in time to the first of the species who feared fire and lightening.

The Renaissance was Florence, and Florence was the Renaissance. Why this should be so is unknown; perhaps the other great sites of the times, Naples and Milan, were too despotic, perhaps Venice too stable; Rome was out of the running because, until the intervention of Jules II, it was Hicksville, dirty, smelly and soiled by papal hangers-on and other such bovines. Traditionally, Florentine merchants vied with each other in their support of the arts. Ghiberti was commissioned to build the doors of the Baptistery of San Giovanni, a task that took twenty years. Brunelleschi somehow capped the Cathedral of Santa Maria del Fiore with a towering roof--the enigma being how the walls of the cathedral can bear the tons of weight--that is still the city's major landmark. Donatello's art seduced Cosimo--as his body did many a Florentine male--who put up with his every caprice. When a merchant refused a bronze head that Donatello had spent a month producing, arguing that a month's labor wasn't worth so much, Donatello sent it hurling from the heights of a tower where it had been taken to capture the best light, all the while protesting that he was an artist, not some laborer paid monthly wages. Cosimo then commissioned a bronze statue of David from Donatello, a hero prized by Florentines because he had overcome the tyranny of Goliath. The result pleases some; for others it is a girlish body with minimal male equipment. Donatello placed his earnings in a basket in his studio and told his assistants to serve themselves with what they needed, but lovers who looked elsewhere were threatened with death by the artist who would run after them wherever they fled, a form of exercise that kept him alive until age eighty.

Today we make an industry of searching each other out; huge amounts of time and energy are dedicated to the enterprise. In Italy sex between males was but a strand of the social tissue. Men worked, studied and played together; they engaged in games and sports and cultural pursuits; they associated professionally or labored side by side. And when the mood and/or occasion was right, they shared a joint orgasm, a way of relief as was playing ball or swimming or horseracing, fencing or tournaments. It was natural in the way that sex should be. It was not the concentrated effort to rack up the greatest number of experiences or glee over the abundance of boys/girls one inseminated. Naturally, sex could become serious; the quest for the girl or boy that one fell head over hills in love with was time consuming and stressful. But the occasional release alongside the buddy who was at hand (literally) was the norm, in the same way that they ate and drank together.

It took the Dark Ages to make sodomy a crime. In ancient Rome male-to-male sex was simply an alternative means to pleasure. Amusingly, the exception to the prohibition of same-sex sex didn't apply to *boys* in Italy, boys could literally do anything they wanted with a male friend. It all fell under the category of 'kids will be kids''. For their parents, sex during adolescence was simply the discovery of one's body: what brought it pleasure, what brought it pain; what worked and what didn't; which zones were erogenous and which weren't. It was discovery—to the adolescent boy far more important than Columbus' fumbling onto the Americas. It was sexuality; it was in no way *homo*sexuality.

It was known that Cosimo's grandson, the great *Il Magnifico* himself, had a marked preference for boy buttocks. The preference was illegal but so prevalent that it was rarely prosecuted. But *rarely* prosecuted still meant thousands of cases that were brought before the courts, which shows the prevalence of the phenomena. A man could be castrated for having sex with a boy (the ultimate cure!); boys 14 to 18 had to pay a fine of 100 lire; boys under 14 paid 50 lire. Foreigners could be legally beaten by whoever caught them *in flagrante delicto*, and if found guilty by a tribunal they could be burned at the stake. In reality no one was much bothered unless he raped a young boy or had sex with children. Consensual sex was more or less admitted; it was the coercive variety that was prosecuted.

Every boy wanted to marry a virgin. So boys who tried to seduce girls could find themselves in mortal danger as families were set on protecting their capital, their virgin girls, girls who served to form the alliances so necessary during the Renaissance. A girl deflowered was no longer an asset. To the contrary, she exposed her family to the open ridicule of the nobility. On the other hand it was accepted that boys needed physical release. The least harmful means of such release was between themselves, a measure that was silently but totally acknowledged.

Naturally, boys could pay for sex in whorehouses or on the street, especially around the old market called the Mercato Vecchio. Alleys at night often saw girls lined up against walls while the boys humped them through the drop fronts of their skin-tight trousers, drop fronts attached by ribbons that could be rapidly untied.

As a banker Cosimo needed papal business due to the prestige that affiliation with the church represented to the world. He therefore cultivated certain men whom he felt might become pope (in the same way he had cultivated the Condottiere Francesco Sforza who eventually became duke of Milan and an enormously important ally). One such man was Parentucelli, a bookworm about whom it was said that anything he did not know was beyond human understanding. Cosimo lent him vast sums of money to buy manuscripts. When Parentucelli became Pope Nicholas V Cosimo helped him found the Vatican Library modeled after Cosimo's own. After Pope Nicholas came Pope Pius II, said to have been the Vatican's first humanist. He nonetheless loved wine, women and honors, all of which Cosimo provided him when he came to Florence. Pius tried to suppress a book he had written as a youth, *The Tale of Two Lovers*, supposedly full of erotic imagery, but through my twenty-first century eyes I see nothing sensual enough to offer the reader. The suppression of the book failed and it was a Renaissance best seller.

Another artist in Cosimo's service was Fra' Filippo Lippi. Headstrong and uncontrollable, his aunt placed him in a monastery when he was fifteen, where he later took his vows. When he discovered that he had a natural gift for drawing, he made his way to Padua to study art. A womanizer who fathered at least one known son, he was forced to flee to Ancona where, out sailing, he was captured by Moors and sold into slavery in Africa. Although human portraits were forbidden by Muslims, he drew the local caliph who was nonetheless so impressed that he freed him. Through the vagaries of life Lippi found himself in Florence working for Cosimo, but his taste for drink, women and bar fighting kept him from his art. In response, Cosimo had him locked in his studio where he ate and slept. He escaped and was found weeks later drunk and whoring. Cosimo tried a different tactic. He sent him into the country where, even so, Lippi met a nun he made pregnant. Cosimo arranged things through Pius II, the pope known for his erotic literature, who allowed the nun and the artist to marry. But before the marriage took place the nun's family poisoned him, although other sources believe he was poisoned by another mistress because of his continued interest in the nun. In any case, he *was* poisoned and Cosimo's grandson Lorenzo had a monument raised to him, built by Lippi's son who had, by then, become an artist just like his dad, Filippino Lippi.

Cosimo the great humanist died, but not before fathering Piero who in turn fathered the great Lorenzo *Il Magnifico*. The image of Cosimo that I love best is reported by an ambassador who, when he visited him, found him in bed between his two sons, Piero and Giovanni, one old man and two others middle-aged, all three suffering from gout.

Cosimo was succeeded by his son Piero called the Gouty, a disease that attacked the wealthy who could afford meat and rich sauces and who disdained vegetables considered peasant food or animal fodder. The result was the retention of uric acid which crystallized in the joints causing incredible pain. Piero married Lucrezia Tornabuoni, a chance for his son Lorenza, the future *Il Magnifico*, because of her forceful nature and intelligence.

Piero was no banker compared to his father Cosimo. He rarely foreclosed debts and loaned funds to the likes of Edward IV of England who battled for years with Henry VI to see which of them would finally become king, running up horrendous bills and then, following victory,

Edward died too young to repay them. Cosimo's squishy-squashy approach made enemies of every class from merchants to the nobility.

Piero attempted to shore up his relations with King Ferrante of Naples by sending Lorenza, superb from the heights of his seventeen years. Lorenzo did more than anticipated, charming the king out of his boots with his youthful candor, intelligence, sparkle and spunk.

In Milan Francesco Sforza died and was replaced by his son Galeazzo Maria Sforza, age twenty-two. Galeazzo had been trained in combat by his father and was therefore feared. When the Duke of Ferrara decided, along with Venice, to take advantage of Piero's weakness as a leader by invading Florentine territory, Galeazzo sent 1,500 troops to Florence's aid. The Duke of Ferrara discovered that, although the citizens of Florence were unsatisfied with Piero, they would not rise up against him as the duke had been led to believe. So he retraced his steps and returned to Ferrara. The Doge of Venice continued on, however, forcing Piero to seek help from not only Naples and Milan, but also from a very feared condottiere, Federico da Montefeltro of Urbino, a city-state on the edge of the Romagna.

Federico da Montefeltro had been trained by Francesco Sforza. A condottiere sent by Venice, the equally feared (but aging) Colleoni, had also proved himself under the direction of Francesco Sforza. Colleoni had, in addition, married Francesco's daughter Battista. Along with Naples, Milan and Urbino, the Florentines themselves rounded up 3,000 soldiers that assembled in the main square of Florence, the Piazza della Signoria, under the direction of the very young Lorenza, in full splendid armor. Galeazzo withdrew his forces for reasons he never explained and so it was that the troops of Federico da Montefeltro and the Venetian troops of Bartolommeo Colleoni met in battle, one that ended indecisively even though both sides claimed victory.

Much has been said about Lorenzo's ugliness, a nose so flattened it deformed his voice and destroyed his sense of smell. It is known that he attracted women who seem to have their own agenda in life's choices. Piero sent his wife Lucrezia to Rome to find a wife for their son. The choice fell on Clarice Orsini, beautiful but scoffed at by Lorenzo's friends behind his back as she was not known for her intelligence. The match was a step up for Lorenzo because the Orsini were nobles well entrenched in the church, many of whom had been cardinals and there had even been one Orsini pope.

Piero, too ill to do so himself, had Lorenzo organize a tournament in celebration of his betrothal, a contest between combatants on horses, armed with lances, aimed at unseating each other. It was said to have cost 8,000 florins while Clarice's dowry had been a modest 2,000 in comparison. There were banners and pennants and Lorenzo himself wore a cloak of white silk lined with scarlet. He rode a white charger given him by Ferrante

King of Naples which made—given the back-stabbing tendencies of Italian politics—Galeazzo Maria Sforza green with envy. The wedding banquet lasted three days, with minstrels, tables laden with roast pig and 300 barrels of the best wine. Although Clarice and Lorenzo may never have been intellectually attuned, they were physically, as she gave him ten children. There is little doubt that more went on in Lorenzo's palaces and stables than girl-boy activities, and it is a fact that the laws against male-to-male encounters were relaxed to the point of near nonexistence while Lorenzo controlled Florence. The artists surrounding him--Donatello, da Vinci, Michelangelo--as well as teachers like the Greek and Latin scholar Poliziano, were homosexuals, as were a number of Lorenzo's closest companions.

Italy throughout the ages, as much today as then, is known for its *jeunesse dorée*. Lorenzo had the best education possible, thanks to his grandfather Cosimo who allowed him to participate in the meetings of the Platonic Academy he had founded. His mother was versed in the arts and Lorenzo spent his life collecting the finest manuscripts, painting, sculptures, coins and jewels--although, again, far less than Cosimo. He loved riding and hunting with falcons, giving full voice to dirty songs that amused his comrades as much as himself. He was not drawn to banking but he had the gift of appointing the right man to do the job in his place. He could be a brilliant conversationalist, an ardent churchgoer, and still slum the nights away in taverns and bordellos, ending the evening in the early hours by serenading the virgin sweetheart of one of his friends—after they had all fulfilled the lustful yearnings of their young flesh. He wrote poems, one of which warned of the ephemeral nature of youth, exhorting himself to make the most of what he had—and he had plenty. Again, then as today: the Italians have always been among the most sensual people on earth, and who could represent the beauty of the era better than the painter Botticelli whose *Primavera* is among the most gorgeous works of the human hand.

Lorenzo was a golden boy, yes, but one who was soon to know adversities that would have brought a lesser man to his knees.

A discussion of the church is necessary to the understanding of the geneses of Alexander VI. For a time the popes reigned in Avignon, a small pleasant town of beautiful fortifications and two beautiful rivers. They moved back to Rome in order not to lose the Papal States, land held from roughly 500 to 1870 when under Victor Emmanuel II Rome was captured as part of the final unification of Italy. At the time of Alexander VI the papacy held sway over a huge portion of Italy. The territory was expanded under two popes. The first pope was Alexander VI, whose reign saw the sudden rise of the ultimate warlord, his own son Cesare. The second was Julius II, during whose reign Cesare met his equally sudden end. The popes had only partial control over the Papal States, their influence varying according to the strength of the lord or count or prince who held this or that papal property.

Depending on the era and the pope, Rome was a dirty town with few inhabitants when compared to ancient times. Much of it was in ruins, the haunt of thieves and murderers, and pastureland filled with goats and sheep. Bands of youths owned the streets, parading where they would, daggers and swords at the ready, beasts with ever-hungry bellies and ever-lustful loins. Cholera and dysentery left corpses where they expired, and the body parts of quartered victims, the remnants of executions, were hammered to doors or, in the case of heads, brandished on pikes. Smelly swamps and piles of refuse polluted the air, a far cry from sweet Avignon.

Pope Calixtus III was a Spaniard who had been in the service of King Alfonso V of Aragon (who also wore a second hat as Alfonso I of Naples). For vice-chancellor he chose his nephew, Rodrigo Borgia, a cardinal at age twenty-five, a Catalan like Calixtus, and the future Alexander VI.

At the death of Calixtus Rodrigo helped to elected the next pope, Pius II, after the usual conclave during which promises of wealth or important positions, such as vice-chancellor, were bantered about in the conclave latrines, the only private area for secret negociations. In thanks, Pius kept Rodrigo on as vice-chancellor, the most substantive function after the pope, one in which a man could gain unheard-of wealth by accepting bribes that covered literally every aspect of human congress, especially sexual, from divorce to incest. Pius tried to limit what the historian Johannes Burchard called his ''endless virility.'' Burchard was responsible for the organization of ceremonies under Pope Pius, and thusly in an excellent possession to claim that Rodrigo organized frequent orgies, one of which, known as the Banquet of the Chestnuts, rewarded those men who had the most frequent orgasms or could ejaculate the farthest, with rich gifts.

The next pope was Eugenius IV, quickly followed by Sixtus IV who kept Rodrigo on as vice-chancellor, again thanks to his work in assuring the pope's election. Rodrigo extended his palace and enriched its furnishings and his clothes. Sixtus awarded him with bishoprics and abbeys, sources of more wealth still. During this period Rodrigo returned to Spain for an extended visit. On his way back his ship was wrecked off the coast of Tuscany and he was taken to Pisa to recover from his close call with death. There, at a banquet in his honor, he met Vannozza de' Catanei, the mother of his future children. In very quick succession she gave him Cesare, Juan, Lucrezia, Jofrè and Otaviano. In return, Rodrigo gave Vannozza a series of complaisant husbands and great wealth. These six were, however, only part of the brood he fathered with other acquaintances.

When Cesare was eight, Rodrigo moved all of his children to the home of his Spanish cousin Adriana da Mila, more qualified to raise them as she was of noble birth and would instruct them in the ways of the aristocracy.

Adriana's son married a beautiful girl known as La Bella whom Rodrigo immediately took as his mistress.

The next pope, Innocent VIII, was known as the Rabbit for his lack of authority. Bands of youths, armed with daggers and swords, ruled the streets of Rome, stealing, raping and murdering to such an extent that the cardinals were forced to place guards with crossbows and artillery at their windows and on the roofs of their palaces. The new pope soon fell ill and died, but not before making Lorenzo *Il Magnifico*'s son Giovanni, age thirteen, a cardinal, a cardinal who would one day become Pope Leo X. The cardinals who came to the Vatican to replace Innocent VII met in conclave, now decided to elect a strong pope who would bring order to Rome.

Following the usual bargaining, during which wagonloads of gold, silver, jewels and precious furnishings and tissues were loaded at the Borgia palace and unloaded at the residences of nearly all of the cardinals (a few were said to have refused the bribes), Rodrigo Borgia became Pope Alexander VI. The truth of the bribes will never be known, and anyway, those who ran against him for pope were at least equally wealthy and equally inclined to bribe whomever they could.

He *was* virile, producing many legitimatized children (as well as being the first pope to ever recognize his bastards) on his main mistress, Vannozza de' Catanei, of whom two were to become world famous, a daughter, Lucrezia, *un véritable four à bites*, as the French say, and a son, Cesare, a veritable--although extremely evil--warrior. He had at least four others he did not recognize officially, but all his offspring and mistresses were abundantly cared for. Alexander was sensual, fun loving, certainly good to his children, a sugar-daddy papa, extremely tolerant, ruthless, courageous, and an administrator of genius.

He and his children spoke Spanish when together, but they all knew Italian, French and Latin. Cesare was destined for the orders, a destiny he hated as he hated his brother Juan who was marked for a military career, one Juan loved but was not good at—or at least not as good as Cesare would show himself to be. Juan was clearly Alexander's favorite, another supposed reason for Cesare's hatred. As virile as his father, slim waisted and certain of his sex appeal, Juan swaggered through the streets of Rome in what can only be described as gorgeous attire, a cloak of gold brocade, jewel-encrusted waistcoats and silk shirts, skin-tight trousers with drop fronts--cloth attached by ribbons that would free a man's loins when he wished to piss. This beautiful, gorgeously clad body, with 30 golden ducats still in his belt purse, was fished up from the Tiber, to the grief-stricken horror of his father who locked himself away from public view for three days. The death freed the way for Cesare to renounce his vows, having been made cardinal at age 18. Alexander never confronted his son with the murder of his favorite boy, but that he was guilty was silently acknowledged by nearly all. On the morning of the murder, just before sunrise, men were seen leading a horse with a body strapped over its back to the river edge, untie and then caste it into the middle. They were accompanied by another man on a white charger, his gold spurs reflecting the moon's glow. The men, said the witness, spoke in very low voices … in Spanish. So it was Cesare … unless … unless, thought some, it was his other brother, Jofrè.

It's not clear at exactly what age Jofrè married but he was thought to be 12 and his wife Sancia 16. As puberty was far later in the Renaissance than today (around ages 15 or 16 then) he was unwilling to consummate the union. His brothers took over the task for him, however, an experience that was not necessarily grueling for the young girl as she was rumored to have had many lovers before arriving in Rome. At any rate, some historians place their bet on Jofrè as his brother's assassin, out of jealously. Jofrè played only a minor role in the uncoiling events attached to the Borgias. At Alexander's death he was made Prince of Squillace, a vassal town of Naples where he lived until he died, having produced four children of his own.

Charles VIII entered Italy on his way to occupy Naples. His stopover in Rome was the first test of Alexander's exceptional intelligence. Alexander withdrew to Castel Sant'Angelo with all his possessions, including his bed. Romans fled to the countryside. Charles tried to calm the Romans by telling them that his men wouldn't take an egg without paying for it. So numerous were Charles' men that they took six hours to file through the gate of Santa Maria del Popolo. They may not have stolen a single egg, but they stole everything else that hadn't been battened down, reportedly cutting off finders when rings refused to budge. They raped any woman silly enough to have not already fled the city. They killed as well, especially the Jews. Alexander finally agreed to a meeting that took place in the papal palace. Charles is reported to have rushed to him and was prevented from a third genuflection by the pope who stopped him in mid-kneeling, giving him the kiss of peace on the lips. As Charles and his troops had brought syphilis, the kiss could not have been hygienic.

Syphilis may have been brought to Europe by Christopher Columbus but this seems questionable as Columbus discovered the Americas in 1492 and the first cases of the disease were recorded in 1494 in Naples during Charles' invasion. How it could have spread so rapidly is one question, another question is why it wasn't present before Charles entered Naples, present in Paris for example. (At that time it was known, in French, as *le mal de Napoli*.) At any rate Charles had it and soon Cesare would be disfigured by its terrible scarification. Luckily for Charles, back in Paris he would knock his head against a doorframe and fall into a fatal coma two years later, at age 28—thus sparing him of the ravages of the disease. But for the moment he's kissing the pope. Charles, despite his extreme ugliness, had at least two different women a day, and in his baggage he carried a book of pornographic sketches and paintings of intercourse with a few select beauties. Alexander successfully bypassed Charles' request that he recognize his claim to Naples, but the French king did insist on having Cesare as a traveling and hunting companion—a hostage to make certain that the pope kept his troops in their barracks. Alfonso II of Naples abdicated in favor of his son Ferrante II who fled Naples, leaving the city wide open for Charles. On the way there Cesare hung back on his horse and then took French leave, leaving the king beside himself with fury.

Alexander had given Lucrezia Giovanni Sforza for husband, but discovering that the boy was a spy for Milan, Alexander decided to annul the marriage in favor of Alfonso of Aragon who was a member of the royal family of Naples and also Sancia's brother. After the slaying of Juan, Giovanni feared that Cesare would kill him too in order to further the ties between the Borgia and Naples. So he easily gave in, especially when he was told that he didn't have to reimburse Lucrezia's dowry of 31,000 ducats. He nonetheless spread the rumor that Alexander wanted the annulment so he could have Lucrezia for himself, and he bruited that he knew for a fact that Cesare had enjoyed his sister on many occasions. When Alexander informed him that he would have to sign a statement saying that he was impotent, he answered that he had had Lucrezia a thousand times (about six month's work for a boy of Giovanni's stamina). As an additional proof of her innocence, Lucrezia was examined and found to be *vergo intacta*. In reality, she was six months pregnant and would give birth to a stillborn child, the first of many such disappointments to follow.

The boy responsible for her pregnancy was a handsome Spanish valet, Pedro Calderon. In a frenzy of rage Cesare chased him through the palace until the lad sought shelter within the robes of Alexander VI himself. The pope tried to protect him but Cesare slashed at the boy through the robes, literally cutting him to pieces. The body was caste into the Tiber.

Alfonso and Lucrezia married and the wedding was consummated.

After the death of Cosimo his son Piero oversaw affairs in Florence, thusly establishing the reality of Medici control over the Florentine city-state. But as he was weak in mind and body, that control nearly ended with him. The city-state of Ferrara, to the north of the Romagna, sent troops to take over Florentine territory, as did the Doge of Venice under the generalship of the condottiere Bartolommeo Colleoni. Florence requested the help of the condottiere of Urbino Federico da Montefeltro. Both men, Colleoni and Montefeltro, had learned their art under Francesco Sforza who died, leaving Milan to his son Galeazzo Maria Sforza.

Once the Duke of Ferrara learned that the Florentines would not rise up against Piero as the duke had been assured, he withdrew to Ferrara. The battle between Venice and Urbino ended in a draw.

Galeazzo Maria Sforza was thought to be a psychopath who didn't hesitate to tear off a man's limbs with his own hands or rape a woman, noble or not. His sexual appetite was hard to appease but once his lust fulfilled, the woman was handed to his entourage for their needs. He detested poachers, strangling one to death on a rabbit pushed down his throat and another was nailed inside his coffin and then buried alive. A priest who predicted Galeazzo would have a short life was starved to death. Galeazzo was finally brought down by three conspirators, one of whom was a very young man named Girolamo Olgiati who, thanks to Galeazzo's library to which the duke gave him access, was able to read the lives of Brutus and Cassius and how they tried to bring republicanism back to Rome through the assassination of Caesar (a perfect example of how the ancient texts formed the Renaissance mind). That was his ideal for Milan. A second conspirator, known only as Lampugnano, had obscure motives concerning land deals. The third conspirator was Carlo Visconti whose sister had been dishonored by the duke, a motive of importance today but at the time everyone was throwing his daughter or wife at Galeazzo in hopes of gaining profit. They met in church. Who struck first is in question, but the version I prefer has Visconti (the boy whose sister was raped) on his knees as if requesting a favor as the duke walked down the nave. When Galeazzo paused to listen to him, Visconti plunged his dagger into the duke's genitals. The other men followed suit. Galeazzo, at age 32, was dead before he hit the ground. The three assassins, certain of public support, did not bother to hide. Instead of thanking them, the citizens of Milan killed Lampugnano instantly and then dragged his body through the streets; the other two were caught later by Galeazzo's guard and their genitals were cut off and stuffed into their mouths before they were disemboweled, quartered and decapitated. As he was dying one of the three is reported to have shouted out, ''Death is perhaps terrible, but honor and glory are eternal!'' Which may be true as I'm retelling the story *500 years* after the event.

Bartolommeo Colleoni, mentioned above, was a Renaissance exception to all of this violence. He was not known for treachery and he didn't rape, nor did he kill without reason. He tended to the vast lands the Venetians accorded him when not leading Venetian armies. He left his fortune to his army and funds to finance an equestrian statue in his honor.

By far the most impressive condottiere of the period was Federico da Montefeltro. He was a Renaissance man, the possessor of a truly wonderful study done in trompe-l'oeil. He's thought to have killed his stepbrother Oddantonio, made easy by the population of Urbino who were unhappy with his reign. Federico took his place as count. He inspired loyalty among his men, sharing his gains as condottiere with them. Because his fees were high, he was able to enrich Urbino. He had surgeons remove part of his nose so that he could see with the eye remaining him, the other having been lost in a tournament. He fought for Florence, for Milan, for Naples and then against Florence before the Treaty of Lodi brought peace to the three city-states. The Treaty ended quarrels concerning the boundaries between the belligerents and confirmed the position of each duke, prince, count, doge or what have you as the head of his particular city. It was not only signed by the three city-states, but also by Venice and the Papal States. The Treaty came to an end with the invasion of Charles VIII on France. After the death of Francesco Sforza, Montefeltro assisted Francesco's son Galeazzo Maria Sforza in governing Milan.

At the death of Piero, Lorenzo was asked by the city nobility to take his place, which he did at age twenty, bowing modestly before the aged men standing before him. His first guest to his palace was Galeazzo Maria Sforza, accompanied by his soon-to-be-famous daughter, Caterina. Unknown to the nobles who requested his leadership, Lorenzo, fearing that he would be brushed aside as being too young and inexperienced, had sent messages to Galeazzo requesting troops, should he be forced to take power through arms. Galeazzo answered by putting a thousand men on the road to Florence. To thank him, Lorenzo put at Galeazzo's disposal every culinary, artistic and erotic pleasure at his disposal. Galeazzo returned to Milan decided to rebuild the city and stock it with art along the lines of Florence. Italy being Italy, Ferrante, King of Naples, became jealous of Lorenzo's influence over Galeazzo. This was Caterina's first visit to Florence, the city in which she would turn to Christ when too old to receive lovers, the city in which she would die.

Lorenzo met with the new pope, Sixtus IV, and is said to have impressed the old man by his youthful vigor, although not enough so that Sixtus would give Lorenzo's brother Giuliano a cardinal's hat (Sixtus did, however, give six hats to his six nephews). Sixtus compensated by giving Lorenzo a splendid head of Augustus to the fury of Galeazzo he wanted it. Galeazzo was becoming less sane each day and, luckily for all, he was soon assassination.

Young Lorenzo's first military sortie was against nearby Volterra that was under Florentine influence, the cause of which was a dispute over trade dues owed Florence. Lorenzo chose the famous Federico da Montefeltro to take the city, which he did, losing, alas, control over his soldiers who sacked, raped and killed hundreds. Lorenzo went to the town to offer his excuses and make amends by handing out money. Lorenzo knew it was a situation that his grandfather and father would have defused before an eventual massacre.

Sixtus IV, who had found Lorenzo to be a darling boy, asked him, as head of the Medici banking system, for a loan of 40,000 florins in order to buy Imola. Sixtus wanted Imola as a gift to his son Girolamo Riario, whom the pope passed off as one of his numberous nephews. Because the pope already owed 10,000 florins to the Medici bank, Lorenzo hesitated, a hesitation that would cost him plenty. The pope, apoplectic, turned to the Pazzi, bankers who immediately agreed. The Pazzi were an old family with money that went way back. The manager of the Rome branch of the Pazzi bank, Francesco de' Pazzi, hated Lorenzo whom he found arrogant and far too rich for a parvenu. He hatched a plan to assassinate both Lorenzo and his brother Giuliano. For this he turned to Girolamo Riario, now lord of Imola, and Francesco Salviati, an enemy of the Medici, whom Lorenzo had forbidden to cross Florentine territory. Salviati wanted to get to Pisa where Sixtus had named him archbishop and Lorenzo's refusal to let him pass deprived him of huge sums of money. The conspirators went to get Sixtus' permission ''to take care of Lorenzo'' which the pope gave, although piously adding that he wanted no bloodshed. The conspirators then went to see Jacopo de' Pazzi, the head of the clan, who refused his consent until he was told that the pope himself had blessed the endeavor.

On the day of the planned murders, Easter Sunday, Francesco de' Pazzi went to the Medici palace in search of Giuliano who said he wouldn't be going to church because he felt ill. Giuliano was an exception among the Medici for several reasons. Although older than Lorenzo, he was never offered a position of real power by his brother. He was far handsomer than the younger Lorenzo and liked to think of himself as a woman killer, which made his entourage laugh because he lacked his brother's charm, meaning that his bed was often empty whereas Lorenzo's never lacked for company. In addition, the youths laughed behind his back because when he did find someone, far from being the heartless enslaver of women's hearts he said he was, he would fall head over heels in love, love that invariably ended with *his* heart broken. Francesco de' Pazzi was accompanied to Lorenzo's palace to fetch Giuliano by Bernardo Baroncelli, a banker and friend of both Francesco and the Medici. They persuaded Giuliano to go to church, giving him a friendly manly hug when he consented—in order to find out if he were wearing armor under his cloak.

In the cathedral Giuliano was separated from Lorenzo by a few yards. Sometime during the High Mass, thanks to a predecided signal, Baroncelli struck Giuliano with his dagger that pierced his brain. Francesco followed with more blows, twenty all together. Giuliano was dead before he hit the marble floor. Nearby two priests attached Lorenzo, one of whom nicked his neck with a dagger, but Lorenzo whipped off his cloak and held it up as protection, his sword already in his hand. As friends came to Lorenzo's aid, the attackers fled. One friend risked his life by sucking the blood oozing from Lorenzo's wound, afraid the dagger had been poisoned. Lorenzo ran to his palace, perhaps believing that his brother, whom he had not seen fall, had already returned there.

The second act of the drama took place at the Palazzo della Signoria, the Florentine Town Hall, a wonderful crenellated tower that overlooks the Piazza della Signoria and the God-inspired statue of Michelangelo's *David*. Here Salviati, the man Lorenzo had forbidden to cross Florentine land so that he could take up his position as archbishop of Pisa, led a pack of thirty mercenaries. Due to the archbishop's reknown, he was allowed to enter the Palazzo della Signoria but due to his incredible nervousness the guards felt that something was terribly amiss. The archbishop was separated from his men who were invited into a nearby chamber that one the guards immediately locked. Government officials sounded the alarm, bells that tolled in emergencies, the ringing of which automatically set in motion the ringing of other bells in other churches surrounding Florence, until the entire countryside knew that something was wrong and, in response, sent armed men to the Piazza della Signoria. The moment the guards at the Palazzo found out what had happened, they killed the thirty followers of Salviati, throwing them from the windows of the crenellated tower. Francesco was found at his palace, badly wounded by a knife blow he had inflicted on himself while stabbing Giuliano. He was taken naked to the Palazzo and hung by the neck from an upper window. Archbishop Salviati himself was flung from the same window, in full vestments. Eerily, he sunk his teeth into Francesco, perhaps in revenge for getting him into such a mess, perhaps to ease the noose around his neck, perhaps due to an involuntary convulsion.

The fifty-seven-year-old Jacopo ran for his life into the country where he was recognized by peasants, arrested, sent to a dungeon and tortured. He was then taken to the Palazzo della Signoria from whose tower he too was hurtled, into space, dressed only in his drawers. His body was cut down and pulled through the streets of Florence by boys beating it with sticks before being nailed to the door of his palace against which they banged his head, yelling out ''Open up, the master is back!'' Other deaths followed, more than a hundred in all as plotters and believed plotters were hounded down.

Sixtus, sick with rage that an archbishop had been hung by the neck in his ceremonial robes, excommunicated all of Florence when the citizens refused to turn over Lorenzo to a papal court. The pope declared war on the city-state and turned to Lorenzo's dear friend, King Ferrante of Naples, for troops which the king provided. The pope named Montefeltro, Duke of Urbino, to head the forces. Now old, the duke proved far less valorous than in times gone by. In the meantime, excommunication had put Florence in the position of a leper, cold-shouldered by its neighbors. Bands of armed youths descended on the city, robbing and raping and depriving it of food. Last rites couldn't be given and the dead couldn't be buried. Lorenzo, seeing that something extraordinary had to be done, took a ship from Pisa to Naples to appeal directly to his former friend Ferrante, a courageous move as Ferrante was as liable to cut off his head as to kiss him. Before leaving Florence Lorenzo had mortgaged his castles and palaces to raise money, money he now spent like water on making gifts to the Neapolitans, on lavish festivals and on charities. It's said, though, that although he laughed at the side of Ferrante during the day, he was in despair at night. Finally Ferrante, faced again with French desires to take Naples on the one hand and, on the other hand, confronted with Turkish ships that were approaching, freed the young man. Also thanks to the Turks, Sextus decided that he needed Florence at his side in his attempt to mount a crusade against them. He lifted the excommunication.

Lorenzo allowed the dissident monk, Savonarola, to preach in Florence where he predicted the imminent death of three dictators, Innocent VIII, Ferrante of Naples and Lorenzo himself. Both Innocent and Lorenzo died in 1492 and Ferrante, at age seventy, in 1494. Lorenzo died relatively young from complications probably due to family gout. He turned over the reins to his son Piero who immediately tried to shore up relations with Ludovico Sforza of Milan who had succeeded Galeazzo Maria Sforza. Ludovico was known to be devious and unpredictable. He had taken a liking to Lorenzo but Piero lacked his father's charm. Ludovico was in fact a regent for Galeazzo's son Gian Galeazzo, but once he'd gained power Ludovico kept it, a fait accompli accepted by Gian Galeazzo who preferred hunting and was considered intellectually stunted. But Gian's wife was Isabella, granddaughter of King Ferrante of Naples. Ferrante sent troops to take over Milan, forcing Ludovico to request the intervention of Charles VIII of France who considered himself the rightful possessor of Naples.

Two years after Lorenzo's death Charles entered Italy at the head of 60,000 soldiers and camp followers, the greatest invasion since Hannibal. His troops, many of whom were mercenaries, were heat-tempered professions, armed with cannons and the morality of beasts. They plundered, raped and murdered their way south. Charles was quite naturally well received in Milan where, under his influence, Ludovico had Gian Galeazzo poisoned, although he spread the word that the young man had died from an excess of coitus. (Perhaps Ludovico had Charles in mind when he made the accusation against Gian Galeazzo for excessive screwing, as the French King had several women throughout the day, and never ever the same one twice, this despite the fact that he was deemed the ugliest man alive.) Alfonso II, who had replaced Ferrante in Naples, fled the city-state. In order to protect Florence from the surge of Charles' barbarians, Piero decided to copy his father Lorenzo by going to meet Charles personally, as Lorenzo had gone to meet with Ferrante of Naples. Alas, Piero was no *Il Magnifico* and Charles, treating him with open disdain, sent him home like a boy. At home the Signoria blamed him for all of Florence's troubles and banished him and his family, bringing down the curtain on the Medici.

In response to the terrible ravages caused by the French, the Italians finally unified in an anti-French coalition sponsored by Pope Alexander VI, noted for his courage. Venetians and Ludovico of Milan took part. Charles was forced to retreat, although in various battles the anti-French coalition lost a reported 2,000 men to every 1,000 lost by Charles. The coalition hounded the retreating French army like wolves, attacking its baggage train until nothing remained to Charles of the tons of gold, jewels and other loot he had amassed. Just a little more than two years later Charles, on his way to a tennis match, struck his head on the lintel of a door and hemorrhaged to death. His successor, Louis XII, decided to follow up an ancient French claim to Milan by launching an attack on the city-state. Ludovico was captured by Louis and imprisoned in an underground dungeon until his death.

Savonarola had welcomed Charles with open arms to Florance, claiming that he had asked God to send the Frenchman as an arm to punish the evildoers in Italy in general, and Florence in particular. When Savonarola had first come to Florence he had gained a huge following because he had had the right answers to how Florentines could wage war against corruption, brigands and iniquity. He painted a clear picture of the depravity of the church, from the trade of indulgences to the selling of cardinal hats. He was the precursor of the coming Reformation, and because he was ahead of his time he was burned at the stake--the word of the true God gone up in flames.

That was not all that went up in flames. Ignorance and superstition took a huge hit when Ferdinand Magellan's crew circumnavigated the world, proving it was not flat. The forces that push some men to do what they do are truly mindboggling, and both Alexander VI and Magellan possessed those forces. In 1494 Alexander VI divided the world in two parts, West of a line that divided the Atlantic down the middle went to Spain, the East went to Portugal. Alexander got the king of Spain to agree to the division and, while he was at it, he gave King Ferdinand and Queen Isabella permission to initiate the Inquisition and rid Spain of Jews and Moors (it must be remembered that Alexander, a Borgia, was himself Spanish). Magellan was a totally fearless warrior, many times wounded in battles against the Arabs. Magellan set out from Seville to discover a route to the Spice Islands, the source of spices that, at the time, far outweighed gold in value. He was given five ships—all totally black due to the pitch that covered even the masts--and 260 sailors, for the most part illiterate scum who thought only of their stomachs and scrotums. They sailed first to the Canary Islands and then to Brazil. During the trip a sailor was caught sodomizing a page. Pages, aged eight to fifteen, were shanghaied to do the menial jobs onboard. The general rule at sea was simply to look away when one was caught in a sex act, the norm being that sailors, in their teens and twenties, took care of each other's carnal needs. For some unknown reason Magellan took offense now, perhaps because the boy was very young. The sailor was garroted (a rope encircled his throat and a stick—called garrote in Spanish—was introduced between the neck and rope and turned until the man was strangled to death). What happened to the lad is unclear. Either he jumped overboard or was thrown; at any rate, he too died. On the coast of Brazil the sailors enjoyed accepted sex with native women, the price being a nail or any other metal object. The crewmembers were careful not to venture far from the ships, as they knew that the natives practiced cannibalism and human sacrifices. The men suffered terribly from heat in summer, as well as from rats and mice that left feces and urine in their food, and lice, bedbugs and cockroaches.

The Straits of Magellan were called, at the time, the Dragon's Tail due to their incredible complexity. To find the passage Magellan had to investigate countless dead ends. Then winter set in. At this latitude winters were terrible: blizzards, storms, howling winds and cold so intense it was a wonder any of them survived. Magellan put the crew on half rations and because no one really believed that a passage existed and because Magellan was inflexible and unfeeling, mutiny was in the air. The first mutiny was foiled because a few crew members, loyal to Magellan, managed to trick the mutiny leading into thinking they were on his side, giving them the opportunity to grab him by the beard and plunge a dagger into both his throat and head. A priest who had taken part was abandoned, in the snow, on an island. Other traitors were mercilessly beaten but not killed as they were needed to run the ships. A few days later, under the cover of night, another ship mutinied by setting a course back to Spain. During my research I discovered an incredible quirk that existed at the time. Saints were listed as being veritable members of the crew! For example, Santo Antonio because he was known to rescue ships; Santa Barbara because she calmed storms. More incredible still, they received a percentage of the profits when the ships returned to port, profits that were turned over to the church.

When Magellan exited the straits he is said to have cried for joy. He was now in the Pacific, a stretch of water, in his mind, less in width than the Atlantic. He would discover that, in reality, it covered half the world, and he was already nearly out of food. Thanks to the Trade Winds, they made it to Guam three months later, although many men were dead from scurvy. They reached Cebu several months after that. Here Magellan became blood brothers with the Prince, both of whom mingled their blood in a bowl mixed with wine that they drank. Ravishing young girls were offered, virgins who had their vaginas enlarged from birth in order to accommodate men who inserted gold bolts through their penises, just under the glans. The tube of the bolts had a hole through which urine passed. The bolted penises were difficult to insert and they didn't allow rapid movements, meaning that intercourse lasted a very long time, even an entire day, and the men could pull out only when soft. The women claimed the bolts gave them ultimate pleasure.

So friendly was Magellan with the Prince that he offered to wage the Prince's battles for him, certain of his superiority thanks to firearms. All the Prince had to do was convert to Christianity, which he did, along with 2,500 of his subjects. Magellan went after those who didn't, so numerous that their poisoned arrows and spears, aimed at the crew's unarmored legs, proved fatal to Magellan and many others.

One ship made it back to Spain, three years after having left, its sails and rigging rotting. Of the original 260 only 18 had survived, among them the ship's greatest treasure, Antonio Pigafetta, an historian who gave us such a detailed account of the voyage that books, based on his observations, have been published, from the time of his arrival to our own day.

That Caterina Sforza was illegitimate was of no consequence in the Italy of the Renaissance. In that, Italy was totally exceptional. Not only was Caterina treated with the same love as her legitimate brothers and sister, she was offered the same education as the boys in the palace, unlike what girls were offered in most other parts of the country. In addition to a superb education, she learned to handle arms, to ride and to hunt. She was a Sforza, born into a family of warriors that dated back to Francisco Sforza, her grandfather. She was thusly the daughter of Francisco Sforza's son, Galeazzo Maria Sforza, whom she adored, and the mother she loved, Lucrezia Landriani. Caterina was destined to be married three times and through each of them she would proudly wear the Sforza name, Sforza meaning ''force'' in Italian. Her love for her father continued untainted even when, at age ten, she was betrothed to Girolamo Riario, count of Imola, who insisted on deflowering her despite the tradition that the girls should be at least fourteen. Girolamo had been offered another girl, age eleven, but her family backed out as soon as they learned of Girolamo's pedophilic tendencies. Girolamo was continuously described at depraved by contemporary historians without further details—although the reason may simply be his taste for virgins and a huge capacity for women in general. Caterina's wedding night may have been rough (as her father certainly knew it would be), but thereafter she was known for her numerous sexual encounters and her attraction to especially handsome lads, one of whom, a stable boy, she raised to lord of Forlì after her husband Girolamo's death. She would eventually present Girolamo with six sons and a daughter.

Girolamo was the son of a shoemaker whose good luck was to have Pope Sixtus, known for his nepotism, for uncle. Thanks to Sixtus IV Caterina became countess of Imola.

Girolamo Riario hated the Medici with every bone in his body because they had always been obstacles in every adventure initiated by the Riario. He therefore tried to assassinate Lorenzo *Il Magnifico* and his brother Giuliano, as we've seen. Girolamo would become known for his cowardliness in battle, and here too, in the attempt on Lorenzo's life, he was not to be found in the heat of things. Only the confessions of the perpetrators made it clear to all of Italy the essential role that was his in the plot. He fell into public disgrace, he infuriated his uncle Pope Sixtus, and he became the object of jokes concerning his bravery and competence. Caterina, at age sixteen, was thought to have lost trust in him.

In rapid succession she had two sons, Ottaviano, whose godfather was none other than Cardinal Roderigo Borgia, and Cesare, named after the great Roman, he who crossed the Ribicon, a river just a short distance from Forlì.

Between Imola and Forlì was the city-state of Faenza, home of the Manfredi and birthplace of Astorre Manfredi, said to be the most beautiful boy in Italy. Imola, Forlì and Faenza were part of the Papal States, territories under the sovereign rule of the pope, and represented his temporal power on earth. Popes had only partial control over the States, some of which were under the command of one prince or another. The hold over Faenza by the Mandredi was backed by the Este family of Ferrara, a country to the north of Faenza, too powerful for the current pope to bring into the Papal States. The power in Forlì, on the other hand, had gone from despot to pope and back again for centuries. At the moment it was in the hands of the Ordelaffi.

Antonio Ordelaffi had come to power in Forlì thanks to Venice. Forlì was a well-fortified city surrounded by walls and surmounted by the nearby fortress of Ravaldino that controlled passage between the north and south of Italy, as well as roads entering the Apennines. The city was passed on to Antonio's son Francesco who was murdered by his brother Pino. Pino failed to take Machiavelli's advice in such cases, he exiled Francesco's small sons instead of strangling them as did the Turks their brothers and brothers' sons. He then went on to poison his wife whom he suspected of infidelity. As she had been born in neighboring Faenza, he gained the enmity of the Manfredi. The next to be poisoned was his second wife and his second wife's mother, both from Imola, gaining him the hatred of the Imolesi. His third bride, Lucrezia Mirandola, was said to carefully watch what she ate. He had no children from any of his wives but did produce a bastard whom he named to succeed him when he fell ill. So hated was he by even his own Forlivesi that he was pulled from his bed still breathing and dragged through the city streets, spat upon and kicked until he was unrecognizable.

His wife Lucrezia became regent for Pino's son but Francesco's boys, now youths, returned to take power. They easily took the city but not the adjoining fortress, Ravaldino, a fortress that would play an important part, later, in the story of Caterina Riario Sforza de' Medici herself. It was within Ravaldino that Lucrezia and her son took refuge. But the boy mysteriously died, giving Pope Sixtus IV the excuse he needed to send in Caterina's husband Girolamo. Girolamo's army chased the three youths from Forlì and now both Forlì and Imola belonged to him and Caterina, count and countess, but not the fortress of Ravaldino. Because it was unbreachable, Pope Sixus offered Lucrezia 139,000 ducats and a new castle if she would leave, which she gladly did.

Caterina and Girolamo visited their new acquisition, a backwater in comparison to Rome (which was, compared to Florence, a slum). The inhabitants were awed by the noble dress of the royal couple, their beautiful horses, the trumpets, flags, banners and pennants.

Now all the count needed was the city-state lying between Forlì and Imola: Faenza. Famous for its ceramics (faience, ergo the name Faenza) and bricks (from which Ravaldino was constructed), it was a land of vineyards and fertile valleys. Its rule by the Manfredi family marks the zenith in its history, a history that goes back to the 1200s when Friar Alberico Manfredi, a Guelph, was put in control of the city-state. Alberico was mentioned in *The Devine Comedy* by Dante as the killer of his cousins. Generally speaking, at the time there were two major parties that stemmed from Bavaria and Frederick Barbarossa, the Guelphs and the Ghibellines. The Ghibellines were an imperial party that supported Frederick Barbarossa in his military incursions into Italy while the Guelphs supported urban liberties. Guelphs were rich merchants in big cities such as Florence and Ghibellines inhabited rural areas based on agriculture.

At the moment Faenza was ruled by Galeotto Manfredi who had the support of his neighbor to the north, Ferrara, ruled by Ercole d'Este. Galeotto's wife was also the daughter of the lord of Bologna. Although Ferrara was powerful and Ercole a condottiere, the powers of the region were clearly Milan, Florence, Venice and Bologna. Ercole was hated by the pope and by Girolamo because of his support of Florence and Lorenzo *Il Magnifico*. As Lorenzo would have been glad to stick a dagger into Girolamo's throat because of his role in Lorenzo's brother's death, Galeotto Manfredi benefited from extremely serious assistance. Girolamo and his only support, Sixtus IV, had to renounce, for the time being, the seizure of Faenza.

Little by little Girolamo became unpopular in both Forlì and Imola. When he first arrived he had freed both states from paying taxes, but soon he found himself near bankruptcy. He persuaded the citizens to vote money to fund 400 guards while in reality he had only 100; he pocketed the difference, an embezzlement that soon came to light. He was haughty and known to swap dirty jokes with his guards in the middle of mass in church.

In Rome he was even more unpopular. Everyone knew of Sixtus' nepotism. Girolamo, the shoemaker's boy, had been named head of the papal guards and six other nephews had received cardinals' hats. All were profligate, one spending, in a very short period, the equivalent of what the war against the Turks cost Sixtus. Old Roman families detested Girolamo's boorish ways and pretention. Only Caterina lived up to what the people expected from a countess and the pope adored her for it. Girolamo, in his soul a thug, knew that the pope had little time left to him. He therefore did everything he could to steal anything he could get his hands on, and send it back to Forlì and Imola. Girolamo sold church offices and demanded money so that those already employed could keep their jobs. The people knew he was a coward because of his role in the death of Lorenzo's brother, and even during the plague in Forlì and Imola, where Caterina had gone from hovel to hovel to bring comfort and priests and what medicines were available to the sick, Girolamo remained in quarantine in his palace, although he did send others, his wife for example, to bring help to the needy.

As Sixtus approached the end, Girolamo put his children into carts filled with furniture, clothing and all the money that hadn't already been expedited, and made his way back to the sticks--Forlì and Imola. The pope's last breath was the signal for his palace and the palaces of his supporters to be ransacked by mobs of the discontented who stole or destroyed what they could, killing nobles foolish enough to hang around.

Incredibly, Caterina hung around too. She seized Castel Sant'Angelo in the center of Rome, while her husband had long since vanished through the city gates.

As head of the papal forces, Girolamo had received orders from Sixtus to defend Castel Sant'Angleo at all costs. Instead, Girolamo had fled Rome but Caterina remained in the Castel and declared that Sixtus' death had changed nothing: Girolamo was still responsible for the Castel until the election of the next pope. This was not possible, however, because the Castel guarded the entrance to the papal palace where the next pope would be named, and Caterina proclaimed that her cannons would blow up anyone trying to get past them. To end the embroglio, the College of Cardinals decided to offer Girolamo, by the intermediary of Caterina, 8,000 ducats if he could get Caterina to give up her hold over them. The College also promised that Girolamo would have continued lordship over both Forlì and Imola as long as he and his descendants lived. For these reasons Caterina agree to evacuate the Castel.

Back in Forlì Caterina found life there and in Imola boring and dangerous. Taddeo Manfredi, who had once ruled Imola, tried, unsuccessfully, to get the town to revolt against its new masters. Both towns were furious over new taxes and duties and both were near bankruptcy. In addition, the weather was dreadfully cold and humid. In March the former ruler of Forlì, Antonio Ordelaffi, sent an assassin to kill both Girolamo and Caterina, a plot discovered in time. The assassin was hanged outside the window of the Girolamo palace as a warning to the citizens of both towns, nearly all of whom now despised Girolamo. Worst still for the population, a new outbreak of plague appeared, giving Caterina another chance to help the needy while Girolamo remained locked inside his rooms, forbidding entrance to anyone. Lastly, Caterina could no longer stand the father of her six children due to his evident cowardliness.

To change air, she decided to visit her mother, sister and relatives in Milan. There, to her stupefaction, she found a city in full bloom thanks to Ludovico Sforza who, against all preconceived notions, had opened Milan to engineers, architects and artists. In fact, the city was being rebuild from the foundations up. The most famous Sforza acquisition was the young Leonardo da Vince whom everyone found gorgeous--slim, strong, physically powerful and possessing cascades of hair flowing around his beautiful face. Caterina anticipated a close relationship by offering the boy a commission to do her portrait. Alas for her, this boy preferred other boys.

Back home in Forlì, Caterina became more and more aware of her husband's unpopularity. She realized that if something happened to Girolamo she would survive only if she were in absolute command of the Ravaldino fortress, said to be impregnable. But the fortress had a particularity. When someone was designated to man it, he was given absolute powers in its defense, and was never ever allowed to go beyond its walls. At the moment the fortress was held by a certain Zaccheo, a person who had bought the job from Girolamo who was always in need of money. Caterina knew she couldn't trust him to turn the fortress over to her in time of great need. Her first priority, therefore, was to put someone else in his place. She rode to Ravaldino, ''pregnant to the throat,'' said Zaccheo when he saw her. Zaccheo told her that he could be replaced only by Girolamo himself, not some woman, be she even a countess and Girolamo's wife. Caterina returned to Forlì and engaged the help of a man who was Zaccheo's only friend, a sinister personage named Codronchi. Codronchi went to Ravaldino and was welcomed by Zaccheo. While awaiting dinner they played cards. When one slipped from Zaccheo's hands and he bent to retrieve it, Codronchi reached for a dagger in the top of his boot and brought it up into Zaccheo's chest and heart, killing him instantly. The man's body was dumped down a well and Ravaldino was turned over to Caterina. Codronchi rode away from Forlì, a much richer man. Tommaso Feo, a stable boy Caterina amused herself with, was chosen to govern the fortress. He came with his brother Giacomo, 15, whom Caterina took an even greater shine to and ... later married.

Things boiled over, and what Caterina had expected finally happened. One of the noble clans, the Orsi, had had enough of Girolamo. As close friends of his, they were allowed to enter the palace early one afternoon while Girolamo was resting, and knifed him. Girolamo was able to raise himself and attempted to get to Caterina's rooms but the Orsi brothers kept slashing with daggers until he lay in a pool of his own blood. The body was thrown over the balcony into the piazza where Forlivesi examined the mangled remains and bloody face. At first fearful, they turned on it once they knew the tyrant was truly dead. He was kicked, spat upon and beaten. The Forlivesi then sacked the palace, taking away everything, down to the bedding. The Orsi ran to Caterina's apartments where she was entertaining her mother, sister and children. The children broke into terrified sobs, only Girolamo's bastard son, Scipione, age fourteen, faced the attackers with bravado. They were all locked in but luckily Caterina was able to get a message out to Naples and Bologna, as well as to the new pope, Innocent VIII in Rome. Bishop Savelli, who happened to be touring the region, entered Forlì the next day and immediately, on learning what was going on, went to make sure that nothing had happened to Caterina and her children. As the population knew that she could count on the huge armies of both Milan and Bologna, neither it nor the Orsi dared harm her. In addition, the mighty fortification of Ravaldino was in the hands of a man loyal to the countess.

Whether Bishop Savelli was in league with Caterina or not is unknown. What is known is that he accompanied her to the fortification of Ravaldino that she promised to hand over to the Orsi. The keeper, in league with her, said he would do so if she would pay his back wages and ensure his future employment there or elsewhere. When she agreed, he said she would have to enter the fortification and give him what he wanted in writing. The Orsi rejected the idea until Bishop Savelli vouched for her integrity. She entered Ravaldino, the door closed behind her, she mounted the steps to the top of the tower where she gave the Orsi--the finger.

The Orsi, outraged, went back to the palace where they fetched her son Ottaviano, age nine. He was brought back before the walls of Ravaldino and a dagger was placed against the lad's throat, the worst possible nightmare for a mother. The child was obliged to cry out for mercy, alerting Caterina to his presence. She returned to the top of the tower and stared down at the Orsi, their troops and the town people who had desecrated the body of her husband and ransacked her palace. She felt she had little to fear as they were all deathly afraid of the consequences of their acts. Spies had already returned to Forlì to inform them that troops from

Bologna and Milan were on their way, and they all knew too that the new pope would never accept that even a hair of any of the children be harmed.

Accordingly, Caterina hollered out the words that have made her famous to this day. She told them all that they could do what they would with her children as she was pregnant again and with *this*, she added, pointing to her loins, she could produce many others. Machiavelli tells us what—or so he wrote—really happened, as was revealed to him by Lorenzo *Il Magnifico*, a friend of Machiavelli. Lorenzo knew Galeotto Manfredi, lord of neighboring Faenza. Galeotto sent a letter to Lorenzo in which he stated that, in fact, Caterina had hiked up her skirt and, pointing to her bare ''cunt'', wrote Galeotto, had bellowed out her famous words. Galeotto's missive to Lorenzo was to make him nearly as famous as Caterina's repartee.

As Girolamo's assassination took place exactly ten years after Girolamo had assassinated Lorenzo's brother, many people felt that Lorenzo had orchestrated it. Unless there's an archive yet to be uncovered, no one will ever know.

Caterina's stance at Ravaldino had a highly unforeseeable consequence. Antonio Maria Ordelaffi, whose family Girolamo had chased from Forlì, had two messages sent to Caterina by arrows shot over the walls of Ravaldino, both suggesting that she and he marry. As the boy was young and handsome, he would soon gain access to her. But for the moment, 12,000 Milanese soldiers arrived to save Caterina. The troops were prepared for battle and for the inevitable sacking of Forlì, their reward. Seeing them, the Orsi brothers hurried to put their threat in action before being forced to flee: they went to kill the Girolamo children. Happily, the children had been hidden away by Bishop Savelli, whose presence had truly been a godsend. The Forlivesi had a sudden change of heart. They now cried out ''Ottaviano!,'' the name of Girolamo's heir, the boy who had nearly had his throat slit. The lad was brought to them, totally mystified by the events that he had in no way been responsible for, and was paraded around the main square of the city three times, symbolizing that he was now accepted as the new lord of Forlì.

When Caterina had regained control, she coolly dismissed the thousands of soldiers who had come to her recue and were waiting to enter and ransack the city. Soldiers always earned part of their pay thusly, an accepted practice recognized by everyone. But Caterina told them, with mind-boggling dispassion and courage, that as the Forlì had stolen everything she possessed, what the soldiers would take in sacking the city belonged, in reality, to her. More incredible still, the soldiers let her get away with it. As for the Orsi, they left Forlì in search of asylum elsewhere and historically simply vanished from the face of the earth. They left their father behind, however, who, at age eighty, was dragged from his bed cursing his sons *for not having succeeded*! His palace was torn down and the old man pulled through the streets tied upside down to the back of a horse, his head smashed to a pulp against the cobblestones.

Galeotto of Faenza didn't have long to snicker over his famous quotation. His wife murdered him soon afterwards. Just being married and having children was normally sufficient for a wife during the Renaissance; a wife's husband's extramarital indiscretions were his business. Women were watched over and chastity belts really existed, especially in Florence, to keep women from unlawful intercourse and from pleasuring themselves. But Francesca Bentivoglio was an exceptional woman whose father just happened to be the ruler of Bologna. Her rival was a beauty known as the Peacock, whom Galeotto was rumored to have secretly married before meeting Francesca, making him a bigamist. Her father knew about the affair and tried to get his son-in-law to mend his ways but failed. When Francesca finally discovered the truth, she fled home, certain that Galeotto would poison her. Through the good offices of Lorenzo *Il Magnifico*, she returned to Galeotto, but only to have him assassinated. The murder was slapsticks comedy, with three assassins hiding under the bed and one behind the bedroom door. In the ensuing struggle it was purportedly Francesca who delivered the decisive blow, a dagger plunged into her husband's chest. But before dying Galeotto had done at least one thing right, he had fathered Astorre Manfredi, as I said, the most beautiful boy in Italy.

Antonio Maria Ordelaffi, who was both young and handsome and had gained access to Caterina thanks to the messages shot over the walls of Ravaldino by arrow--in fact, he was at that very moment able to appreciate her ... cunt ... from close up--, immediately offered Francesca his hand in marriage, Bologna being infinitely more desirable than Forlì. Bologna laughed at the offer but decided that with Galeotto dead it was the perfect time for it and Milan to send troops to bring Faenza over to their sides. Lorenzo *Il Magnifico*, although an ally of Milan, didn't want the Milanese to extend their control so far to the south. Lorenzo lacked troops but not intelligence. He spread rumors about Faenza being sacked by the troops from Bologna and Milan, the troops outside of Forlì, the troops that Caterina had prevented from entering her town. They were now ready to descend on Faenza, said Lorenzo, rousing the inhabitants into action. The outcome was chaos that Pope Innocent VIII ended by issuing an edict, in 1488, confirming three-year-old Astorre Manfredi as lord of Faenza and named an eight-member regency of noble citizens to care for the lad and the city-state. The boy had now embarked on the world stage. His mother, Francesca the assassin, remained safely in Bologna. At the same time that little Astorre was made prince of Faenza, the child Ottaviano was confirmed as ruler of Imola and Forlì, under the regency of Caterina.

Humanism played a great part in the education of the young Astorre. It consisted of classical authors, especially Cicero, and included studies in philosophy, history, rhetoric, grammar, mathematics, poetry, music and astronomy. Based on the Greek ideal of a sound mind in a sound body, it included also archery, dance and swimming. There was hunting, which boys took to naturally. Humanists insisted on the genius of man, on morality and on the extraordinary potential of the human mind. Schooling was for rich boys but places were available for poor students of recognized ability. A model education combined the classics with the basics of Christianity. Once a boy developed himself intellectually and physically, he was in the ideal position to become an ideal man, as well as having prepared himself for the best possible afterlife. Latin as well as Tuscan vernacular were in usage. Dante wrote his works in Tuscan Italian, as did the wonderful Boccaccio. One of Caterina's lovers, Pietro Bembo, helped establish Tuscan Italian as the language of the entire peninsula.

Erasmus was named the Prince of Humanists. Before the arrival of humanism men believed in eternal salvation after death, but philosophers such as Erasmus preached the enrichment of life in the here and now. According to him, the church had to free itself of superstitious and corrupt behavior. It had to drop its pomp, relics and beads used as magical charms. Cults based on saints and indulgences, the purpose of which was to make money by reducing the time believers would spend in hell, had to be proscribed. (One priest was fond of telling people that as soon as a coin rings in the bowl, the soul for whom it is paid will fly out of purgatory and wing straight to heaven.) He fiercely believed in free will, without which human moral action would have no meaning. He accused monks, priests and popes of living in luxury after taking vows of poverty, of caring for their own needs before those of their flocks. Life began in the womb, he wrote, and one shouldn't be baptized until old enough to accept Christ. He believed that lust was a natural body function like the need to eat. He denounced those who waged war as beasts and he pitied the stupidity, ignorance and gullibility of the ''faithful''. Erasmus favored circumcision. (He would have been better off letting boys decide for themselves, after puberty, as he did for baptisms.) While on penis-related subjects, I can add that he is idealized by gay groups for being homosexual; heteros furiously deny it. This reminds me of those historians who believe that the Borgia should rot in hell for their iniquity, while others make a saint of Alexander VI. The truth, naturally, is that no one will ever be certain one way or another about either Erasmus or Alexander.

Thanks to Gutenberg's press, Erasmus' books were known far and wide. Nearly 4,000 pages could be produced by movable type per week compared to several pages that were hand copied. Erasmus could thusly publish thousands of copies of his books, making him a best seller (750,000 of his works were sold during his lifetime alone). The advance was due to three factors: the use of the screw press, known since antiquity and used for crushing grapes and olives; the invention of metal type, in this case finding a perfect alloy consisting of lead, tin and antimony (which gives type its hardness); and the proper ink, which was oil based, more durable than water based. Gutenberg's press played a key role in the dissemination of knowledge to the masses, breaking forever the monopoly of literacy held by the nobles. By year 1500 there were 77 cities throughout Italy that had printing shops.

Erasmus formed a long friendship with Thomas More, a supposed humanist whose reputation was muddied by the six executions for heresy during his chancellorship. More was against the Reformation which cost him his life under Henry VIII who died in his bed in terrible pain, small retribution for the thousands of woman, boys and men he'd had hanged for one reason or another.

It's of interest to know what else was going on in the world at this time, a time especially harsh on boys. In 1485 the English king Richard III gave orders for his two nephews, Edward V (who had just been crowned king), age 13, and his brother, Richard Duke of York, age 9, to be smothered to death in the Tower of London. According to Alison Weir's wonderful book *The Princes in the Tower*, the boys certainly suspected what awaited them, as they had grown increasingly melancholy. Then, suddenly, they ceased appearing at the windows of their chambers. Richard was given a summary burial at his death, due to his role in the murders, and has been despised throughout history ever since, giving both Shakespeare and Sir Lawrence Olivier moments of creative glory. There can be no more heinous crime than the killing of children, and what awaited Astorre and his brother was even worse as they had marks of torture on their bodies and both were said to have been abused sexually before being thrown into the Tiber.

Despite the fact that Cesare had murdered his brother and Alexander's favorite son, Juan, both father and the remaining son, Cesare, now formed a tandem (it is difficult to count the insignificant Jofrè), the purpose of which was to extend Alexander's power and to give Cesare enough strength so that he would be able to replace the pope, at his death, becoming the first ruler of a unified Italy since the Romans.

To get things going, Alexander arranged a rapprochement between Louis XII of France and the Vatican. This the pope accomplished thanks to three of the new king's needs: the need to conquer Milan; the need to reconquer Naples, lost with the death of Charles VIII; and the need for a divorce so that Louis could marry Charles' widow. Louis offered Alexander a huge sum of money and gave Cesare, whom all recognized as the new rising star, the duchy of Valence. Cesare would also be given command over several thousand French troops. Satisfied, Alexander threw in a cardinal's hat that the French had requested for years. Not to be outdone, Louis raised the stakes by offering to find Cesare a noble wife.

When Cesare realized that he would soon be meeting Louis in person, he decided to turn himself into a perfect male by force of exercise, physical exercise as well as exercise in arms and horsemanship. He spent hours at the task and contemporaries agreed that there was not a finer looking Italian in all of Italy, with the exception of Astorre Manfredi who began to draw artists and sculptures to Faenza to capture his face for eternity. The artists who flocked to do Astorre honor wielded an art that was reborn, one that took its roots in humanism and in classical antiquity. It was based on classical texts rediscovered thanks to the likes of Cosimo de' Medici and thanks to commissions by the powerful Julius II. It was accompanied by technical advances that improved the quality of oil paint adopted by Titian, Tintoretto and Uccello. Da Vinci perfected the art of painting thanks to lighting and perspective, as well as incredible detail in anatomy and landscape.

Cesare's face may not have equaled the beauty of Astorre's, but his good looks were increasingly disfigured by the ravages of syphilis. The syphilitic rashes, euphemistically called ''flowers'', came and went like the tide, leaving him handsome or disfigured *selon*. He took to wearing masks during his bad days, the effect of which enhanced the fear people already had of him.

When the time came, Cesare set off for France with cartloads of precious gifts. He was beautifully dressed in black and white velvet, pearls and gold chains and precious gems attached to his clothes and boots, his horse was attired in gorgeous livery and silver bells. In addition, he had not forgotten the cardinal's hat to be presented to Georges d'Amboise, Louis' trusted counselor. Cesare was offered the sister of the king of Navarre, sixteen-year-old Carlotta. Louis wrote Alexander a description of the wedding night, telling the pope that Cesare honored his wife eight times in a row. Louis added that he had done the same with his new wife—thanks to the divorce Alexander had accorded him—but confessed that he had nonetheless done less well as his sessions had been broken up, twice before dinner, six times afterwards. Alexander replied that he was awed by the king and proud of his son but not surprised by his virility. Carlotta was immediately pregnant. Charles' former wife wasn't.

As Louis XII's troops descended into Italy, Ludovico Sforza fled Milan with all the booty he could carry and Frederico did the same in Naples, choosing the island of Ischia for his exile. Ludovico was later captured by the French and spent the remaining years of his life in prison, Frederico was awarded a pension and died in the French town of Tours.

Now that Alexander and Cesare were aligned with France against Milan and Naples, Lucrezia's new husband Alfonso, illegitimate son of the former king of Naples Alfonso II, was an embarrassment that the two men eliminated by eliminating Alfonso himself. The boy had dined with the pope and was on his way home when waylaid by men with daggers. Wounded, he was taken to the Vatican where the pope gave him his own rooms. Instinctively knowing what was in store for the lad she loved, Lucrezia hovered over him day and night. Alfonso knew who was responsible for his injuries, and when he had recuperated enough, he took a potshot at Cesare with a crossbow as he passed through the garden below Alfonso's window. Cesare was unscathed, but his reaction was immediate. He sent men to clear Alfonso's rooms of both Alfonso's sister, Sancia, and his wife, Lucrezia. When they refused to budge, the men told the women that they were acting under orders from the pope himself. If the two women doubted their word they could ask the pope who was in an adjoining apartment. As they left to do so, the doors to Alfonso's rooms were closed and Alfonso strangled. Cesare made no pretense of innocence, maintaining that since Alfonso had tried to kill him, he was only protecting his life.

Cesare then left Rome at the head of thousands of French troops and headed for the Romagna and the city-states he was set on conquering in the name of the pope because they were, after all, Papal States. On his way he visited his dear sister Lucrezia who was recuperating at Nepi after the loss of her beloved Alfonso. One wonders what they had to say to each other….

One of the men accompanying Cesare was the artist Pietro Torrigiano. His story is singular because Torrigiano was a sculptor under the patronage of Lorenzo *Il Magnifico*. He is credited with bringing the artistic segment of the Renaissance to England where he finished out his life. But through a quirk of human nature, he is known today as the man who broke the nose of Michelangelo. Torrigiano had been one of Michelangelo's lovers and, in a fit of jealousy, smashed the great artist in the face. Knowing how furious Lorenzo would be at his disfiguring Michaelangelo, Torrigiano fled. As Cesare was offering money to new conscripts, and as Torrigiano needed money, he joined his troops. Later he would become renown for sculpting the memorial to Henry VII of England, a man as atypical as Torrigiano.

From Nepi Cesare went on to Rimini to capture the city-state from the Malatesta. The Malatesta were a family of hotheads, schemers and murderers who ruled Rimini from 1295 until the arrival of Cesare who extinguished them with the ease of blowing out a candle. The first Malatesta was a hunchback, Giovanni, who killed his wife Francesce and his brother Paolo when he discovered them in flagrante delicto.

The Malatesta were often condottieri in the service of other Italian city-states. The most famous was Sigismondo. He took up arms at age 13 and became lord of Rimini at 15. He murdered his first wife and was known for his treason, first against the pope, then against the Sforza, the Florentines and finally the Neapolitans. After drowning his second wife he succeeded in betraying Siena, Venice, the Sforza for a second time and Florence again. Pope Pius excommunicated him for acts of sodomy on his own son. He was also accused of incest with his daughters, also par for the course during the period. Most of the above city-states raised troops to get rid of him, under the direction of Federico da Montefeltro. He fled to Venice where the Serenissima, who never did anything like the others, took him in. He plotted to assassinate the pope but returned home instead to peacefully die in his bed.

On his way back from Rimini Cesare came upon the sister of the ruler of Rimini whom he had just chased from power, the grandson of Sigismondo. Cesare immediately sequestered and raped her over a period of months, denying any knowledge of her whereabouts. Anyway, he scoffed, he didn't need to rape women as they came to him willingly from everywhere. Which was true. Ambassadors from many city-states were nonetheless so upset by the abduction that they joined forces in demanding that Alexander severely punish his son. Alexander too was reported as being upset, but in the end, what could he do? The woman was eventually restored to her husband but from what she reported later, either she was suffering from Stockholm syndrome or her months with Cesare hadn't been all that traumatizing.

The time had come for Lucrezia to marry again, a marriage which would, naturally, benefit the pope. Alexander thusly chose the son of Duke Ercole of Ferrara, another Alfonso, Alfonso d'Este, for his daughter Lucrezia. Behind closed doors the Duke of Ferrara laughed at such pretention. His family was noble, old and wealthy, that of Alexander hick parvenus. Ercole had heard stories about them all, that Alexander had prostitutes from the best bordellos brought to him after dinner, that Cesare slept during the day and whored at night, that both he and his dad had shared Lucretia, that they were murderous slime, socially nonexistent and morally rotten to the core.

Yet … his own boy was perhaps no better. Alfonso was known to have two interests in life, making cannons in his own personal foundry and parading around town at night, his sword in one hand, his erect cock in the other. His former wife had been so fed up with him that she turned to women for satisfaction. Stories of incest, sodomy, rape, murder, *et j'en passe* may seem exaggerated, but personally I believe they represent just the tip of the iceberg. The repressive atmosphere during the deep darkness that followed the fall of Imperial Rome was such that when the light finally came, when the period known as the Renaissance finally rose from ancient Rome's ashes, the liberation--intellectual, artistic and sexual—was such that Italy knew few bounds. And this liberation came to a people that just happened to be among the most beautiful created by the fertile mind of God.

But the wedding did take place since Louis XII of France wanted it, all because he needed the Borgias to further his ambitions. The price Ercoli demanded would have been dismissed out of hand by any other person in Italy, but not Alexander who disposed of literally bottomless resources, resources brought in, in multiple ways, every single day, via every church in the country. Alfonse was 26, Lucrezia still only 21. Parties were thrown in Rome prior to her leaving the city, one of which, in 1501, was the famous Banquet of the Chestnuts described, during which prizes were given to those who could come the most times and copulate with the most prostitutes. Some say Lucrezia was present. Some put Cesare there. Others, like Puzo in his *The Family*, place them both. All name Alexander.

The trip to Ferrara and the celebration there cost a fortune, but the wedding night came off well. Alexander was told that Alfonso had contented Lucrezia that night and then took his pleasure with other women during the day. The pope supposedly thought this just fine as Alfonso was a young man and, as such, multiple adventures were good for him. The historian Burchard wrote that all the talk of lubricity inspired the pope to increase the number of prostitutes he welcomed into his rooms that night. As always in Italy, love was indeed in the air.

In Forlì love was also in the air. Caterina decided to see Antonio Maria Ordelaffi. Their relationship lasted months, during which the Forlivesi happily anticipated the coming marriage. After all, Caterina, decided and intelligent as she was, was nonetheless a woman and as such needed male direction. (No matter what she accomplished, the idea that she depended on men would hold true until her death.) But Caterina had other ideas. She had had her eye on a stable boy, Giacomo Feo, since he was fifteen. Now seventeen, tall, lithe and supranormally handsome, his contemporaries tell us he was big where it counted. When Caterina found herself pregnant, she secretly married the kid.

All hell broke out in every direction. Forlivesi and Imolesi couldn't accept the primacy of a stable boy over their cities, and Bologna, Milan, Florence and Ferrara proclaimed that they had youths of noble birth who could satisfy the countess at least as much as Feo. The city that eventually won out, should Caterina choose one of their boys, would not only broaden its territory thanks to its influence over the two city-states, but it would control a major artery through the Apennines. Foiled attempts were made on the lives of both the countess and her lad, but she brought her pregnancy to term, giving birth to a baby boy, Bernardino. The marriage and the baby were kept secret because she did not want to undermine the ascension of Girolamo's son Ottaviano. She thusly decided to end any rumors concerning one or the other by punishing the rumormongers. She had them systematically beaten, many of whom were permanently maimed and at least one was killed. But it was a wonderful period for Caterina. A visiting ambassador was allowed into the inner sanctum of Caterina's palace where she and Giacomo were playing with Catherina's children by Girolamo and her son by Feo. He described the husband and wife, in the light of the setting sun, as pure angels.

In 1492 two major events occurred. Lorenzo *Il Magnifico* died, bringing an end to the golden age of the Italian Renaissance, and Roderigo Borgia became Pope Alexander VI, the warrior pope who would, in his way, also aid in the demise of the Renaissance. (Naturally, 1492 was also known for Columbus' discovery of the Americas and the year Magellan germinated the idea of circumnavigating the world.) Caterina was thrilled as Alexander was the godfather of Ottaviano, the heir of Forlì and Imola. The new pope raised troops against the invasion by the French king Charles VIII. Alexander requested Caterina's help which was refused. In reality, Giacomo Feo, the stable boy, now decided politics for the two city-states, certain that he knew as much or more than seasoned kings, counts, ambassadors and other diplomats. But Alexander hadn't gotten where he was for nothing: he put two and two together and offered Feo 16,000 ducats for his help, which Feo accepted. When the French under Charles finally got to the Romagna they took the town of Mordano, defended by Caterina's troops. The town fell to far superior forces and Mordano's army and citizens were raped and murdered down to the last one. The massacre was such that Caterina immediately swung over to the French side, earning the enmity of the pope, Florence and a good number of other states. An ambassador traveling through the region declared, after meeting with Feo and Caterina, that she would gladly forfeit anything, Forlì, Imola, even her own children--she would, in fact, sell her very soul to the devil or give up all her property to the Turks--rather than lose her precious Giacomo Feo.

It was now 1495 and her son Ottaviano, age 16, was a man. In an attempt to gain what was his, he went up to his mother and Feo and demanded to be recognized as the new count of Forlì and Imola. An argument ensued that ended with Feo slapping the boy who stormed out of the room red-faced. A week later, as Feo was riding through the woods along with Caterina, a group of friends approached them on horse. As Feo chatted amiably with one, another stuck a dagger in his back. Caterina had the presence of mind to turn and ride off to the impregnable shelter of Ravaldino. Feo's bodyguards also took flight, leaving the handsome boy to fall from his horse into a ditch.

The people of Forlì remembered the heads Caterina ordered cut off after the assassination of Girolama. So when the murderers of Feo came riding into the town square, their clothes filthy with his blood, shouting to all the account of their exploits which, they maintained, were designed to give power over Forlì and Imola to their rightful count, Ottaviano, a group of nobles thought best to go to Ravaldino to find out what had really happened. When they returned, they ordered the arrest of the assassins. The reprisals were indeed terrible. The murderers had their heads axed open, from the top to the chin. Their wives and mistresses and children were slaughtered. Their houses were torn down brick by brick. Two babies associated with them, age three and nine months, along with their nurses, were bludgeoned to death. An accused priest was dragged behind a horse, his head fractured against the cobblestones, as Caterina had ordered done to Girolamo's assassin, old man Orsi. Under torture another conspirator gave out the name of her son Ottaviano, known by all to have hated Feo for usurping his rightful place as count of Forlì and Imola. Caterina had her son arrested, an act so horrifying that the inhabitants followed the boy to the gates of Ravaldino where Caterina dispersed them with cannon fire. After a stormy meeting with his mother, the boy was put under house arrest. At Feo's funeral all of Forlì and Imola turned out, so afraid were the populations of their countess. Heaven entered the act by bringing down a plague on the people: rashes appeared on their genitals and their lymph nodes swelled up. The syphilis epidemic had begun. Caterina ordered her palace torn down because it had sheltered both her and Feo, and his statue in bronze was raised in his honor. A new palace was build on the grounds of fortified Ravaldino. Its furnishings and gardens were so exquisite that Caterina called the place Paradise. She sent Ottaviano to Florence to learn the art of war. The sixteen-year-old lad, a veritable Don Juan like his father Girolamo, left behind mistresses and bastards.

Caterina had eight children. Bianca Riario was her only girl and Caterina destined her for the handsome Astorre Manfredi of neighboring Faenza. All the surrounding powers had their say in the matter, some for and some against, but the negatives and positives equaled themselves out. For Caterina the union of the lad, age ten, and the lass, age fourteen, would unify the region, as Faenza was exactly in the middle between Forlì and Imola. Faenza was ruled by a Council which was doing an excellent job of both educating the young Astorre and of governing the tiny city-state. A pretender, however, Ottaviano Manfredi, Astorre's cousin, decided that the time was ripe for him to take power from the boy who was still a child. The resulting disorder attracted the attention of Venice who was always on the lookout for an easy kill. Bologna came to the same conclusion, as did Milan. All three decided to descend on Faenza. The brouhaha dissuaded Caterina from pursuing the marriage with Astorre and it was therefore annulled. Bianca would finally find a suitor, a count from the region of Parma, when she attained the ripe old age of twenty-two.

For Caterina, marital bliss occurred much sooner. At age thirty-three she fell in love with Giovanni de' Medici, thirty, perhaps the first veritably educated man in her life, who was also handsome and charming and, said one wag, a boy for whom she would kill father and mother to keep near her.

They were secretly married because of Ludovico of Milan's enmity towards Florence. Knowing that he would find out anyway, Caterina tried to soothe Ludovico's anger by naming her only child with Giovanni, Ludovico Sforza de' Medici. Incredibly, her new husband Giovanni had inherited, in spades, the ills of his ancestors: he died in Caterina's arms, probably of complications due to family gout. In his memory she renamed her child Giovanni Sforza de' Medici.

That Caterina's private life was in shambles didn't mean she couldn't try to find happiness for her children. So when Alexander VI, her son Ottaviano's godfather, suggested a marriage between the boy and Lucrezia, Alexander's daughter, she knew that this would be the first step in turning over Forlì and Imola to the pope. Such a marriage could also turn out to be disastrous for her boy, Ottaviano. Caterina remembered that Lucrezia's first husband had been declared impotent after three years of marriage despite the boy's outcry that he'd had her ''at least a thousand times,'' and the fact too that he'd fathered bastards. So to protect her boy Caterina refused Alexander's offer, and in the nick of time too. The next candidate, Alfonso, was strangled on Cesare's orders.

Alexander decided on the direct approach and sent Cesare to bring Forlì and Imola into the lap of the Papal States. Caterina put the finishing touches on the defenses of Ravaldino just as Cesare arrived at the head of an army of twelve thousand of Louis XII's French troops. After promising her money and a palace of her own in Rome, the tone between the two-- Cesare on his white charger facing the drawbridge to Ravaldino, Caterine atop the crenellated tower--turned sour as one insulted the other. They split up but after a few hours of reflection Cesare returned. This time Caterina was standing on the drawbridge. Cesare dismounted and approached the edge. Luckily for him, he was in beauty that day. The terrible traces of his syphilis had temporarily disappeared. Handsome and gorgeously dressed in black velvet, a rarity during the period when both sexes preferred bright colors (after the austerity of the Middle Ages), he decided to trade the filthy language he was partial to with the troops (similar to today when, in the locker room, it is impossible to hear a single sentence without the obligatory insertion of fuck) for the sparkling oratory of the likes of Cicero. Caterina too was in beauty, her breasts propped up by a tight bodice. She was immediately aware that Cesare had come to seduce her with a stunning smile similar to that used by Stanley Kowalski to mollify his wife Stella. Caterina, with the same intention, turned a welcoming shoulder in his direction, he held out a hand to touch it, she enticingly took a step back in the direction of the door to Ravaldino, he followed … until he felt the drawbridge rising under his feet. He jumped off just in time to see Caterina disappear behind the closing door. Cesare, his face red with shame for having been tricked, stormed off.

Sadly, Cesare would win out. What Caterina had pointed to when the Orsi had put a dagger against the throat of her son when ordering her to surrender Ravaldino, what Galeotto had referred to as her "cunt" in a letter, would soon be not only his, but his until he himself felt that his humiliation of her had gone on long enough. (Although some writers during the period suggested that she grew to *like* Cesare and his form of humiliation. Naturally, we'll never ever know.)

At any rate, Cesare immediately went back to his obscene military language and ordered an all-out attack on the citadel. I won't go into the actual destruction except to say that she was betrayed from inside the walls, walls opened to Cesare and his French troops. The Italians inside were spared but ransomed; the mercenaries under Caterina had their throats slit. She stepped over seven hundred strewn corpses on her way out of Ravaldino, in time to see her monument of bronze to her beloved Feo being carted away prior to being melted into cannon balls. Feo was symptomatic of what had undermined her place in Forlì and Imola: she had fought for her own pleasure and a place in the sun for her children; she had known hundreds of lads and wealth and luxury beyond measure; and so as one citizen summed it all up as she was hauled away, "She had put her faith in herself and in the walls of her fortress, and none in the people she ruled".

The French commanders observed the fate of the women left behind, their thighs spread as the men lined up. They knew that the prettiest had already been put aside for themselves later on. Realizing what was in store for Caterina, several tried to save the countess by telling Cesare that they had precedence over her and would assure her safety right up to the moment she came before King Louis XII. This hiatus ended in an exchange of money. Cesare retired with the countess while the French officers, rich, sought the comfort of the naked forms awaiting them under the covers of their own beds. One of them was heard to say, as he unbuttoned his superb military jacket, "Well, at least she won't be wanting for sex."

As with all seventeen-year-olds, Astorre Manfredi had everything to live for. Of medium height, with a boyish chest and slim waist, his eyes were blue and his hair as blond as gold--curly waves of which descended to his shoulders. He was courteous, had a good word for everyone, and was as aware of his charm and sexual appeal as is every Italian boy, then as today. His family had ruled the city-state of Faenza for two centuries, and although there had been some bad apples, the Manfredi, in general, had done somewhat better than the other lords, dukes and princes. of the Romagna. Astorre himself was loved. Although the real power behind Faenza lay with the Council that had been regent since Astorre Manfredi was named lord at age three, he had his word to say and that word was listened to more and more frequently. Faenza was one of the few veritable free spirits to exist outside Florence, and it was more of a republic than even the Florentine city.

Indeed, Astorre had everything to live for, and perhaps even a bit more as he had received the best education available. Private tutors had instructed him in Latin, even if his daily speech was in the Italian vernacular. He had read Homer and Plato, the Greek tragedians, Suetonius and Xenophon and Plutarch, he had studied the texts of Cicero and was himself on the road to becoming an accomplished speaker.

Puberty had come later than it does today, but he had already known girls and women. In fact, his extreme beauty brought blushes to the maidens in the market; today he would star on American Idol. His marriage to Caterina's daughter Bianca had fallen through but it was of little consequence as there were plenty of other matches to be made with girls from far more important towns than were Forlì and Imola.

Faenza was well fortified, but its strategic location meant it was in continual danger from this power or that. Like the atomic bomb today, Faenza, being surrounded by powers such as Bologna, Milan, Florence and Venice, was in a strategic position because if one power dared to attack, the others would tear it to pieces in order to maintain the status quo. Faenza was fortified, but with Cesare prowling around the region the citizens of the city-state decided to add to their fortifications and ensure that neighboring cities would come to their succor if and when needed.

Astorre's first appeal for support went to neighboring Bologna. After all, his mother was the sister of Giovanni Bentivoglio, the lord of Bologna. Bentivoglio sent a thousand troops to Faenza but was later forced to withdraw them due to pressure from the French king Louis XII and also the pope who threatened excommunication. Louis thanked Bentivoglio for the withdrawal by taking Bologna under his wing, thus preserving the city from future ravages by Cesare. The pope also sent a note of thanks. As a sign of further capitulation, Bentivoglio agreed to feed and house a number of Louis and Cesare's soldiers. Astorre appealed to Venice, a power he could usually depend upon, but Venice too was afraid of Louis and besides, when Louis overran Milan he gave certain lands adjoining Venice to the Serenissima who was now in his debt.

When Cesare did more than prowl, when he attacked and ravaged neighboring Forlì and Imola, Faenzans were armed and readied for action. At first Cesare tried charm. He met with the Council and with Astorre, informing them that the time had come for Faenza—like Forlì and Imola—to return to the lap of the Papal States under the direction of their pope, Alexander VI. Nothing would change other than papal troops being stationed in the fort, in addition to Faenzans being enrolled in the ever-more-numerous papal armies. Astorre and the Council didn't accept Cesare's offer, as he probably knew they wouldn't, but it gave Cesare a chance to weigh them both. He loved the boy as did the Faenzans, and he was known to bed lads that caught his fancy, a bent that amused his men, many of whom shared the same drift.

Cesare had far bigger fish in mind than tiny Faenza but he couldn't just bypass it. It was at the entrance to the Apennines and it controlled an important route, the Via Emilia. Anyway, if he let a little fish get away, just because he liked the ruling prince, what chance would he have with bigger states? So he attacked. To his immense surprise the Faenzans defended themselves tooth and nail, even the women took up arms. Priests melted down sacred objects to provide money. The wealthy gave up their stocks of wheat and wine. The siege went on and on until the coming of winter, the winter of 1500, more than normally cold and snowy. Leaving enough men to make certain that Faenza wasn't supplied in food and weapons, Cesare went to spend winter in Cesena, a locality he liked so much he was thinking of making it, when all power was in his hands, the capital of the Romagna. He spent money like water, offering games, tournaments and processions, and organized huge festivities at Christmas and during Carnival. He showed his prowess by challenging the local boys to wrestling matches and horse races, all of which made him immensely popular. His admiration for the people of Faenza was such that when a merchant escaped Faenza and came to Cesena with important information concerning which parts of the walls were the less secure, Cesare had the man hanged.

With the coming of spring, in March to be exact, Cesare returned to Faenza where he bombarded the walls of the city for five months, concentrating on the spot revealed by the Faenzan traitor. As food and water were lacking and the dead were piling up, as there were fewer stones and hot pitch to cast down on the invaders, Astorre and the Council were obliged to seek a truce. Cesare had no reason to give the Faenzans anything. Victory was his. But he did like the lad, and it had always been his policy to be as lenient as possible with a population. In that way he could count on the defeated to provide him with food once they had returned to the fields, as well as to give shelter for his men and horses and furnish the cannon fodder necessary to win battles. In addition, the Council paid him personally 40,000 ducats. So, good-humouredly, he offered the boy what he wanted, and the boy wanted everything. He wanted Faenza free of foreign troops, he wanted Faenzans to be able to keep their possessions, and he wanted Cesare to forbid sacking and rape. All Astorre had to do in exchange was sign over the town to Alexander VI, which he and the Council agreed to do.

Astorre and his fifteen-year-old brother Gianevangelista were given their freedom, but to Cesare's astonishment they wanted to accompany him to Rome, as today kids want to see the lights of New York. Both boys also deeply admired the most virile, courageous and experienced warrior in recent Italian history. To learn from him would make them men on the way up; Cesare was their elevator to the very top floor. It was a fatal mistake because bright lights rarely come without the accompanying greed, vice and corruption that carpet the walls in shadows, as the French say.

The year was 1501. Caterina was taken to the Castel Sant'Angelo from whose walls she had, sixteen years earlier, kept the cardinals from the conclave needed to elect the next pope. She deeply regretted those she had murdered after the assassinations of Girolamo and Feo, a score for the first, two score for the second. Life supposedly meant little at the time, yet I remain convinced that individuals during the Renaissance wanted to live out their lives, just as we do today, to the last moment. They certainly were barbarous, hanging people until they were nearly dead and then cutting them down, still alive, so they could watch themselves be disemboweled or have their hearts cut out still beating, or, the horror of horrors, have their privates cut away and stuffed in their mouths to suffocate on. The rape of women was an essential perk of war, as was ransacking and destruction. Children died unnecessarily, some before the eyes of their parents. So Caterina had reason to repent and beg for God's forgiveness. We certainly have reason to be thankful for our own more civilized times ... if, naturally, one excludes the Great War responsible for 20,000,000 deaths, the Second one that caused twice that, and more recently the slaughter of 8,000 boys over the age of 13 in Srebrenica, all of whom certainly begged for their lives right up to the last horrifying second.

Caterina was taken to Castel Sant'Angelo and locked away out of the reach of those like Cesare and his close friends who would be able to crow over having possessed the charms of the Cleopatra who hadn't gotten away. Her pain deepened when she discovered that her sons, Ottaviano and Cesare, were doing just fine under the rule of Alexander, from whom both boys sought the red hat of a cardinal. With mistresses and bastards galore, they were certainly on the right path to seeing their wishes fulfilled. News from Florence informed her that her last husband's brother was dilapidating the fortune Giovanni de' Medici had willed to her and his son, little Giovanni.

At age ten Caterina had visited Florence with her father Galeazzo Marie Sforza and had been welcomed by Lorenze *Il Magnifico* himself. Thanks to the intervention of Louis XII, who respected her as a ruler and as a warrior, she was freed from Castel Sant'Angelo--after signing over Forlì and Imola to Alexander. As she left the castel she crossed paths with Astorre Mandredi who was being imprisoned. The year of his imprisonment was 1501. She made her way back to Florence, the most beautiful and cultivated city of the Renaissance, where she would die. In an ending that was almost a fairytale of beauty, she was met there by her sons Ottaviano, Cesare, Galeazzo, Sforzino, and Carlo--the son of Feo. Her only daughter, the loyal Bianca, was also waiting for her, holding in her arms little Giovanni, the son of her last love, Giovanni, whose fortune his brother had not entirely dilapidated--in fact, there remained enough so that Caterina could live in comfort and offer sums to her sons who never ever stopped making requests for this and that, just as they had, when infants, lustily and eagerly suckled at the breasts of their wet nurses.

To save her soul she made donations to convents and churches, especially to the convent of Muratte where she asked to be interred. These donations were to Christ, for it is to Christ that women turn when they are no longer of an age to welcome virile lovers. She passed away at age forty-six. The year was 1509. Her tomb was desecrated 300 years later and her remains lost; Muratte became a prison.

But before we finish with Caterine, perhaps just a word about her last son, little Giovanni, son of Giovanni de' Medici. Different from the other Medici, he spurned intellectual activities in favor of martial interests. He often ran away from home and liked the company of simple farm boys. At age twelve he killed a boy from a rival gang Giovanni had formed, and at age thirteen he raped a boy of sixteen. Trying desperately to save him, Florentine nobles put him under the control of an ambassador, Salviati, who was named to Rome. There Giovanni slummed with lowlifes, in perpetual trouble. He became a condottiere and was known for exclaiming, ''I rule with my ass in the saddle and a sword in my fist!'' Pope Leo X chose him first to police Rome and then to form an army using men of normally irredeemable depravity that only he had the force to make into manageable soldiers. He specialized in lightening strikes with a preference for ambushes. His motto was, ''I embrace my rivals in order to strangle them.'' When his patron Pope Leo X died, Giovanni added black stripes to his armor, for which he is known historically as Giovanni dalle Bande Nere. He married Salviati's daughter and had a son destined to become lord of Florence. Severely wounded in battle, he had to have his foot amputated; ten men were needed to hold him down. He died five days later of gangrene. He was the very last of the condottieri. Of his direct descendants, other than fathering a Florentine lord, one, Marie de' Medici, became Queen of France--but led a terribly sorrowful life. (The Florentine lord he sired was Cosimo I who would rule Florence, whom we'll discover in the life of Michelangelo.)

For Cesare, Caterina, Forlì and Imola were an interlude to much bigger acts of bravura. We went on to take Urbino, the citadel of the Montefeltro and a dozen other city-states. Along the way he heard stories about some of his captains, traitors in the pay of Roman nobles eager for the reign of Alexander to come to an end by assassinating their leader, Cesare. He invited them to a dinner at one of his palaces and on an agreed signal troops surrounded and dispatched them all. He moved on to Siena, sacking, destroying, maiming, killing and raping. Those who wouldn't give up their money were tortured; if they were found to have nothing to give up, their throats were slashed (the soldiers were instructed that this was the best way not to blunt a sharp sword or dagger).

Cesare was no fool. He knew his father would not live on forever. He had thusly looted Italy of every ducat confiscatable, he had storerooms of weapons at his disposal and his troops loved this handsome fearless man who conceded their every wish as long as they remained loyal to him. What he didn't count on was *his* nearly dying at exactly the same time as his father, which is precisely what happened. What he didn't count on either was the election of a new pope as vigorous, intelligent and belligerent as Alexander had been.

He and his father had been invited to a banquet after which they both fell seriously ill. Illness was nothing new to the Renaissance. I haven't gone into the subject, but all the actors in this book, all without exception, had fallen ill multiple times throughout their lives. Lucrezia, for example, could nearly be described as being continuously sick—especially following her many miscarriages. Illness came from literally everywhere, bad food, incredibly diseased water that one drank or swam in; illness came from common flue, from typhus, cholera and malaria; from flees and rats and dogs and other people. Illness came through breathing, sweating, defecating and fucking. Illness favored the months of July and August, hot muggy months propitious to dysentery. All of Alexander's predecessors, Innocent, Sixtus, Pius and Calixtus had died during those months. And it was now July and both Cesare and Alexander were at death's door. Perhaps they believed, as did the people, that they had been poisoned during the banquet. Perhaps, as some said, they themselves had tried to poison their host--an ever-criticizing cardinal they both could well do without--but somehow they had drunk their own means of murder. As Alexander was now seventy-three, he was in more danger than his young son. They were both bled although, unlike his father, Cesare was plunged into cold water, the accepted cure for fever. Alexander received last rites but not Cesare, a former cardinal, who vaunted his atheism.

Alexander did die. The year was 1503. Was he guilty of some of the most heinous crimes known to humanity—even, as we shall see, the buggering of Astorre Mandredi and his fifteen-year-old brother before ordering them to be strangled and thrown into the Tiber? Or, as one recent source claims, did he die a misunderstood saint? There is only one response: God will know His own. Let Him decide who goes into the eternal flames or who gets access to the 72 virgins. As for me, I've spent a lot of time reading about this unique creature without whom—and without miscreants like him--history would be a far more boring concern. But … one doesn't touch children. If Alexander had harmed Astorre, if he did survive until the ripe old age of seventy-three (and he did), if there is no eternal punishment, if death is, in fact, just eternal nothingness, if, in a word, there is no justice for boys as innocent as Astorre and the 8,000 Srebrenicans, then I do have to ask myself, Just what is all this fuss on earth really about?

Nearly overnight Cesare lost it all. His palaces were sacked and the lands he had conquered were recovered by the counts, lords and princes he had overturned. He was carried away by litter to recuperate at his sister's retreat of Nepi. In Rome Pius III was elected but immediately passed away, replaced by the powerful Julius II, a mortal enemy of the Borgia. Strong in body and mind, intelligent, handsome, arrogant and utterly ruthless, the new pope had contracted syphilis but with age he replaced the lust of the loins with that of the stomach, devoting himself to roast pig and strong wines. He created the Swiss Guard and put Michelangelo to work on the Sistine Chapel. He refused Henry VIII's divorce, ending the Catholic Church in England, and he brought war and peace to the continent according to his whims, and was only prevented from uniting Italy into one country by the emergence of someone still more powerful than he, the Grim Reaper. The year was 1513.

Julius issued a warrant for the arrest of Cesare, accusing him of the murders of his brother Juan, his sister's husband Alfonso, Astorre Manfredi and Astorre's brother, as well as many others. But in exchange for his giving up the wealth he had horded and the fortifications in the Romagna still in possession of those who remained loyal to him, he was allowed exile in Spain. He retired to Chinchilla, a mountain castle in the heights near Valencia.

Cesare's rout was such that even King Louis XII, who had called him his dear son, sent word to Ferrara and Alfonso, Lucrezia's husband, that he was free to leave her as France no longer recognized her as being his legitimate wife. Luckily for Lucrezia, Alfonso had grown to love her, and this despite the fact that she had never stopped welcoming lovers into her bed. Other scandals continued to haunt her. One of Alfonso's brothers, Ippolito, who happened to also be a cardinal and was known for his unbounded lustfulness, had fallen in love with a local beauty. The girl claimed that she far preferred another of Ippolito's brothers, Giulio, whose beautiful brown eyes alone were worth more than all of Ippolito. In response the cardinal waylaid his brother and tried to cut out those wonderful eyes. Alfonso forced Ippolito to ask for pardon, but as Giulio suffered horrible pain and the near total loss of sight, he decided to get revenge on both brothers, Alfonso and Ippolito, by having them killed. He united his forces with still another of his brothers, Ferrante. Their conspiracy was discovered, however, and although Alfonso would not have them executed, he did send them to prison. Ferrante died in his dungeon forty-three years later, Giulio endured for another fifty-three.

Caterina gave herself to Christ; Lucrezia, despite ever-increasing amounts of donations to convents and churches as she grew older, never abandoned that part of herself that wanted to be a woman to men of flesh and blood. Right up to the end she continued affairs with men, the two most important being Francesco Gonzaga and Pietro Bembo, for whom she wrote letters of stupefying sensuality (for the period).

Right up to the finish line she continued to give Alfonso children, five in all, of whom three were the precious boys who would assure that the name d'Este would live on in a plethora of youths to this very day. At age thirty-nine she died, (the year was 1519), giving birth, birth to a child and birth to a star, her star, that shines as brightly now as it did 500 years ago, solid proof that it is better to use life and be used by it than to flee the storm, dodging the droplets, seeking an illusive shelter that exists, in the end, for none of us.

In the mountain retreat of Chinchilla things turned badly for Cesare when his exile turned into captivity. Isabella of Spain decided to follow Julius' lead in prosecuting him for the deaths of his brother Juan, duke of Gadía, and Lucrezia's husband, Alfonso of Aragon, both of Spanish lineage. He escaped, climbing down a rope. He made his way by boat and trek to Pamplona in Navarre, to his brother-in-law Juan of Navarre who put him at the head of his troops. As the city-states in Spain were in constant upheaval just like their Italian counterparts, Cesare was constantly at war. His last day found him chasing a band of rebels. At age thirty-one he was still in the full glory of his bravado and virility and so thought nothing of outdistancing his men. Alas, the rebels he was chasing turned to face him and, highly outnumbered, he received many blows, one of which was the fatal plunge of a dagger to his throat, just above the armor. He fell into a ravine, just like Catherine's stable boy husband, Feo; he was stripped naked as Feo had been; but his genitals had not been mutilated, as Feo's--his were covered by a rock by one of the attackers who recognized him. Juan of Navarre had the body buried in the small church of Viana where it lies to this day. Cesare often compared himself to that other Caesar, and as they died nearly on the same day it can perhaps be said for one as for the other: *Aut Caesar, aut nihil*! -- Either Caesar, or nothing! The year was 1507.

In the spring of 1501 a new prisoner was added to Castel Sant'Angelo on the very day that Caterina was freed. Astorre Manfredi, her would-be son-in-law, had lost the town of Faenza to Cesare after a brave defense. He and his brother Gianevangelista had accompanied Cesare to Rome to learn about life and war. But unlike Caterina, the young nobleman had not earned the admiration of the French and was consigned to the lowest cells.

In 1502 the unfortunate boy suffered the fate that Caterina escaped: he was strangled in the prison and his body dumped into the Tiber. Johannes Burchard wrote that both boys had been participants in an orgy along with a large number of very young girls. Whether they freely consented to take part or were forced to will never be known. Whether the orgy even took place will never be known. Cesare was said to be involved—it would have been far from his first. Perhaps his father took part too. Burchard only says that "a certain powerful person sated his lust" on the boy. Many historians say the bacchanalia never happened. Machiavelli gets into the act too because he was there, physically there to give Cesare advice, one piece of which we find in his book: "When a prince assumes power over a conquered territory his first obligation, if he wishes to preserve that power, is to destroy the rulers in place." Every time, in Italian politics, that this principle hadn't been observed, the prince lived to regret it. Turks systematically had their brothers garroted as their very first act on ascending to the throne. It's true that had the boy lived he might have eventually become a problem for Cesare. But a more likely eventuality is that Astorre, already immensely popular in his hometown, might have outshone Cesare himself in public adulation, an intolerable risk to a man who wore impeccable black velvet and paraded around on a white charger adorned with bells, his stirrups made of gold.

Burchard says that Astorre and his brother Gianevangelista were fished from the Tiber, attached together with a stone tied to their necks. The bodies of the aforementioned females were also discovered, tied together in the same fashion. The boys' bodies had torture marks. Cesare pushed his fiendishness to extremes by greeting an envoy from Venice and springing on him the news of the murders, knowing that Venice had taken a special and highly favorable interest in both Faenza and Astorre Manfredi. The envoy was said to have not even blinked, unsurprising for a city where slaves could still be purchased, their prices varying from six ducats for a man to a hundred for a beddable girl. Burchard ends his story by saying that "The young man was of such unequaled beauty and intelligence that it would be impossible to find another as sterling as he in all of Italy." The boy was 17. The year was 1502.

PART III

BOTTICELLI
1445-1510

At that time in Florence there existed special letterboxes that citizens used to denounce other citizens. It was in this way that Botticelli came to the attention of the authorities. He was accused of "keeping a boy." An investigation took place but as ironclad proof was unavailable the charges were dropped. As he was now well known and visibly had only a few more years to live (six, as it would turn out), the Office of the Night responsible for such cases turned a blind eye. His reputation didn't seem to have suffered as afterwards he was appointed to decide where Michelangelo's *David* would be placed in Florence, housed to protect it from the elements or, as Michelangelo wished, outside in view of all in the splendid Piazza della Signoria. It was decided to put it outside, but the original was later replaced by a copy so that the original could be protected inside—although, by then, a madman had taken a hammer to its toes, in 1991.

The incomparable beauty of Botticelli's art is such that his sexuality is not of even tertiary interest. Perhaps if he had been a really bad boy as Caravaggio, or of sublime beauty, surrounded by sublime beauty as was da Vinci, my attitude would be different, although it's true that the self-portrait of himself in his *Adoration of the Magi* is exquisite. He later turned towards the cretin Savonarola who had nonetheless served an important role in giving Italians of all classes direction—in his case spiritual direction—in times of terrible turmoil. He burned part of his gorgeous oeuvre, to our eternal loss (if true, which is doubted by some). The great Guicciardini in his marvelous *Storie fiorentini* tells us more about Savonarola: ''There were no more games in public, and even at home they were played in an atmosphere of fear. The taverns, which had been the meeting places for all the rowdy youth who enjoy every vice, were all closed up. Sodomy was ended and women abandoned showy and lascivious clothing, and young men resolved to live in a saintly and civilized way. They went to church regularly, wore their hair short and cast stones and cursed dishonest men, card players and women who dressed in lewdly. They went to the carnival and collected all the dice, cards, paintings and corrupt books, and burned them publicly in the Piazza della Signoria. Savonarola brought help to men who abandoned pomp and vanities, and restricted themselves to the simplicity of a religious and Christian life.''

He came into the world as Alessandro di Mariano di Vanni Filipepi, in Florence but was called Sandro. Botticelli means ''little wine barrels'' and was applied to his flabby brother, although for some reason the name spread to the whole family. As with Verrocchio and many other artists, he too began as an apprentice goldsmith. At age 17 he was admitted into the workshop of Filippo Lippi (we followed Lippi's far more turbulent life in Part II) who taught him perspective and techniques in fresco, as well as the beauty of pale colors in contrast to the brighter palate that Botticelli favored. Luckily Botticelli entered the service of Giuliano de Medici, later assassinated, as we saw, in Santa Maria del Fiore. Under the protection of Lorenzo *Il Magnifico* and Medici patronage in general, he became famous and rich, and enriched our lives and knowledge by producing paintings of

Lorenzo, Giuliano, Cosimo, Piero and Giovanni de' Medici. Then Savonarola entered the stage and a part of Botticelli's works went up in smoke (again, supposedly, as Vasari doesn't say a word about the bonfire), followed by Savonarola himself, burned at the stake.

His paintings are to be discovered in situ in museums, a wonderful reason to travel throughout Italy, and a wonderful place to make acquaintances (where I met my very first lover, in the Salle des Vases grecs in the Louvre, the story of which can be found in my *HOMOSEXUALITY – Volume Four – Modern Times*). As my purpose here is not to evaluate art—which is also far beyond my competence—I can only repeat what we all know, which is that the *Birth of Venus* and his *Primavera* are irreplaceable masterpieces (and the lad on the far left of *Primavera* is to die for). Later modern-day Savonarolas tried to cleanse him of a homosexual stain by maintaining that the Venus in the *Birth of Venus* was an unrequited love, Simonetta Vespucci, who sat as the model—it turned out that she had been dead for years.

Incredibly, he went into an artistic eclipse due to the eminence of Michelangelo, da Vinci and Raphael, but reason won out and today he is firmly in the firmament of da Vinci and Michelangelo. He did little painting after Savonarola's bonfire of the vanities, most of which were on the lines of ascetic religious themes. It's true that the bonfire occurred in 1497 and his great triumphs years earlier, *Primavera* in 1482 and the *Birth of Venus* in 1486. At his death he was poor and unaccompanied to his final resting place.

SIXTUS IV
1414-1485

Upon being named pope, Sixtus IV made six of his nephews cardinals, at least one of whom was his lover. Another of his lovers (but not a nephew), Pietro Riario, was appointed cardinal, and at his death the inscription on his tomb stated that he had gained renown for "his loyalty to Sixtus and gift of spirit and body." At the time "body" supposedly meant that Riario had been well-endowed. The historian Stefano Infessura called him "a lover of boys and sodomites" who awarded benefices and bishoprics in exchange for sexual favors. In all, he nominated thirty-four new cardinals, his illegitimate sons as well as handsome boys who had sexually gratified him. One of his nephews, but most probably his son, Raffaele Riario, was named papal chamberlain.

It is known that Sixtus fathered children, one of whom, Giuliano della Rovere—later Pope Julius II—was born in incest with Sixtus' sister Raffaela della Rovere, with whom he may have had other sons too. Giuliano was named cardinal at age 18, and was said to have also had incestuous sexual relation with his father.

Infessura maintains that for the love of a barber's boy, age 12, Sixtus named the father to a high papal position and awarded the child with riches and a bishopric.

Sixtus authorized the Spanish Inquisition and confirmed the rights of the Portuguese to practice slavery among non-Christians. To compensate for (or dissimulate) his Tartuffery, he wrote learned religious texts, bestowing on him, at the time, the reputation among the people of being pious and devout.

He arranged the marriage of his nephew Giovanni della Rovere to the daughter of Federico da Montefeltro (fully discussed in Part II), thereby founding the line of della Rovere dukes of Urbino.

Sixtus kept Rodrigo Borgia as vice-chancellor, which put Rodrigo on the fast track to becoming Pope Alexander VI. He met with Lorenzo *Il Magnifico*, "a daring boy," he said, who impressed him with his youthful vigor. When the daring boy refused to give him 40,000 florins so that Sixtus could buy Imola for his son Girolamo Riario, the pope flew into a rage, becoming instantly open to a plot by the Pazzi, a noble family in Florence for whom the Medici were vulgar parvenus, to assassinate Lorenzo. They succeeded only in killing Lorenzo's brother Giuliano. One of Sixtus' archbishops was in on the plot and when caught was thrown, in full vestments, from the window of the Palazzo della Signoria. Sixtus excommunicated Lorenzo and put Florence under interdict until Florentine men and money were needed in Sixtus' war against the Turks, at which time the interdict was lifted.

The Sistine Chapel took its name from Sixtus who saw to its restoration, as well as employing Botticelli to paint his frescoes, the *Temptations of Christ*, the *Punishment of the Rebels* and the *Trial of Moses*. He ordered the construction of the Sistine Bridge (Ponte Sisto), the first built since antiquity. He favored dissection of human corpses, those of both criminals and those unidentified, and is thought to have given his nod to 27,000 executions over a two year period. He insisted that the University of Padua, where he had been a student, maintain its independence from the church.

And then Sixtus was implicated in the story of Simon of Trent: In 1472 the father of a missing boy went to the authorities and frantically reported that his son had not returned home that night. Search parties were sent out, and as they found nothing, the father demanded that the houses of the Jews be searched, as an itinerant preacher, Benardine of Feltre, had recently given a sermon vilifying the Jews and their use of children's blood in the preparation of Passover matzo, as well as in other rites. The dead body of the boy was eventually found in a ditch, drowned. Eighteen Jewish men and five women were suspected of the drowning and put to torture by *strappado*, explained in Part II. Some confessed their guilt, others didn't.

When Sixtus heard about the affair he had the proceedings stopped until his representative, Bishop Dei Sindici, had time to arrive. The bishop found that the Jews were innocent but mob violence forced him to leave Trent. Nine of the prisoners were burned at the stake, although a tenth, age 80, had time to commit suicide. Two others converted, which allowed them exactly one more day to live, followed by death by allegedly more humane beheading. The child became the focus of veneration and the bishop of Trent tried to have him canonized, especially as over a hundred miracles were attributed to him within the year of his death. This took place in 1475. Simon was declared a martyr by a later pope, Sixtus V. In 1758 the Jews were formally cleared by Pope Clement XIV. In 1965 Simon was removed from the Calendar of Saints.

PART IV

RAPHAEL
1483 - 1520

The first thing to known about Raphael comes from Vasari: ''So gentle and charitable was Raphael that even the animals loved him.''

The second key is found in those around him, beginning with his student and lover Giulio Romano who became known for 32 drawings called the *I Modi*. Sixteen represented scenes of heterosexual intercourse, 16 others of homosexual couplings. The first 16 were reproduced by the engraver Marcantonio Raimondi and gained such notoriety that they were banned and destroyed under the order of the pope. But they had been more or less well copied by others and can be found today on the Net (you won't be impressed as they're pretty dull—the copies, at least). The 16 homosexual drawings were considered too outrageous to be copied, and so have been entirely lost. The first 16 came to Shakespeare's notice: In *The Winter's Tale* Queen Hermione mentions, ''that rare Italian master, Julio Romano.'' Besides these, he did some beautiful paintings, for example his *St. John the Baptist in the Wilderness*, a beautiful young boy *à la da Vinci*. His *Jupiter Seducing Olympias* is an oddity, Jupiter's fully engorged penis just inches away from insertion.

The second personage associated with Raphael is Pietro Aretino who wrote dirty sonnets to go alone with the *I Modi*, but is especially known for his satirical writings, so sharp, witty and revealing that Charles V and François I paid him blackmail under the guise of patronage so he wouldn't include them in his satires. He was, if you will, the talented Renaissance Walter Winchell (known by millions but himself so unpopular that only three people attended his funeral). Aretino too was unpopular with hoards of Italians, barely escaping assassination on several occasions.

The third man is Federico II Gonzaga of Mantua. Mantua, beautiful but dull until the arrival of the Duke, became a center of art, as had Milan under Ludovico Sforza, a vulgar condottiere until he visited Lorenzo *Il Magnifico* in Florence. Seeing the splendor of Lorenzo's court and the magnificence of the city—where, after all, the Renaissance began—Ludovico had an epiphany. Back home, he changed the face of Milan, architecturally first, then artistically, bringing aboard da Vinci himself (as we've seen). Frederico was so afraid of Pietro Aretino that he literally became his pimp in procuring boys, as witnessed in this highly-abbreviated exchange of letters that Federico wrote to Aretino, in answer to a request: "I would willingly satisfy your wishes regarding this kept boy who you write could remedy your trouble, if I knew who it was, but I do not know this boy Bianchino." The Duke finds out who the boy is and writes back: "I truly love you more than any other and the fruits of your splendid intellect have so impressed me that I will never forget them. If I could possibly satisfy your desire for Bianchino I would do so gladly. But having understood his reluctance when I spoke to him on your behalf, I did not think it fitting to plead with him or otherwise to exhort him, and I surely can't order him, it not being either just or honest to command him in this case. So pardon me if I have not pleased you. If I can in any other way, you know very well I am only too glad to do it and you will always find me ready...." It was true that boys who sold their favors could gain not only money but a position in the upper hierarchy of government or church. It was true then as today: Clark Cable, wrote William Mann in *Wisecracker*, let himself be fucked by William Haines in order to get a role, and Darwin Porter in *Paul Newman* claims that Newman automatically opened his fly when he saw a certain glint in a director's eye.

Aretino had said of himself: "I was born a sodomist," and it was true. But like all Renaissance men (who normally had a more or less hidden weakness for boys) he too had a weakness, but in his case it was with a woman, a cook. As he wrote Giovanni de' Medici: "My Illustrious Lord, be absolutely assured that I will return to my old ways, and that when I escape from this madness with a woman I will butt-fuck an untold number of men, for me and for my friends." One wonders how he could possibly have had this kind of conversation with Giovanni if Giovanni hadn't shared Aretino's tastes. It's extremely strange to read these letters from civilized highbrows who spent their time screwing boys, boys who were well paid, I hope, for what they had to endure from these fat, powdered miscreants.

Raphael Sanzio (or Sanzi or Santi) was born in Urbino in 1483, the fief of Frederico da Montefeltro whom I've already discussed at length. His father was a court artist and it was at court that Raphael, young, learned proper manners and social skills. He was helping his father at age 4, thanks to which he progressed in talent (as did the equally young Mozart, years later). Of that time Vasari says that the boy "was a great help to his father." His self-portrait at age 16 shows a boy of unsurpassed beauty. He was apprenticed very early, some say around age 8, to Pietro Perugino, "despite the tears of his mother," states Vasari. Around age 11 he went to Florence for 4 years and then around age 15 he went to Rome where he lived until his death, 12 years later. It was there that Pope Julius II put him to work on several Vatican rooms, in one of which he painted his most famous work, the huge mural *The School of Athens* showing da Vinci, Raphael himself, Sodoma (more later) and Michelangelo sitting in front. Here we have the trinity of the times: the Everest of men, da Vinci, followed by the world's Annapurna, Michelangelo, and Raphael. Of da Vinci Raphael said that the moment he saw his works, he gave up all previous knowledge to devote himself to his new master. Raphael was present at the Vatican during the time Michelangelo painted the Sistine Chapel, visiting it during the artist's absences. When Michelangelo found out, he accused Raphael of undisclosed "plots" aimed at him, as well as for copying his works. No one, and especially not Raphael, denied that he copied the works of others, copying being a way of growth. Michelangelo hated da Vinci too, but the challenge was in finding someone the creator of the God-inspired *David* didn't hate. At any rate, Raphael didn't follow Michelangelo into stilted mannerism which, happily, had an early death.

Julius II sent two of Raphael's paintings to François I for reasons of diplomacy and allowed Raphael to do a painting of him, which is sad because the warrior pope comes out looking deathly frail and sick, the antithesis of what he was in earlier life where he lived for war, boys, food and girls, in that order.

Raphael's *Baronci Altarpiece* was seriously damaged by an earthquake but fragments exist, of great beauty, as is the portrait of Giulio de Medici, the future Pope Clement VII, who is seen in the painting *Leo X*. But his *chef d'oeuvre* is *The School of Athens*. Along sexual lines, he was summoned to adorn the Vatican sauna with erotic paintings, in a room called the Stufetta, one of which shows the randy goat-god Pan leaping from the bushes with a valiant erection.

Raphael opened his own workshop with, says Vasari, fifty apprentices and assistants, among whom were his lovers, Giulio Romano and Gianfrancesco Penni. Thanks to these men Raphael was able to produce an amazing number of paintings. They all looked as though they had come from the hand of the master, but in reality many cooks had been involved. Raphael was especially noted as someone who would take over the techniques of others, incorporating any and all external influences. He was also a perfect collaborator, establishing peaceful relations between men of extremely varied characters.

After Raphael's death Giulio Romano and Gionfrancesco Penni continued his workshop, their inheritance from Raphael. One of their assistants was Caravaggio. Unfortunately, they separated and died apart. Raphael died of fever, at age 37, supposedly after a night of excessive lovemaking with a mistress, all of which leaves one dubious, as if claiming that Tchaikovsky was heterosexual because he married—twice. (Although Renaissance men *did* dip their brush, as the French say, into both sexes.)

Pietro Bembo, known, among other things, for his love affairs with Caterina Riario Sforza de' Medici, as well as the notorious Lucrezia Borgia, wrote this on Raphael's tomb: "Here lies the famous Raphael by whom Nature feared to be conquered while he lived, and when he was dying, feared also to die." Raphael would most certainly have preferred a more modest epitaph. He was buried in the Roman Pantheon, one of the very rare monuments remaining from ancient Roman times. A hundred painters accompanied the procession, carrying torches. A man deeply loved and revered, his tomb is of incomparable eminence and splendor ... "for an artist," said one contemporary.

JULIUS II
1443-1513

I won't go into the life of Alexander VI as it was thoroughly covered in Part II. Julius II was different from the other popes, with the exception of Alexander, in having balls, big brass balls like those shown peeking through the waist-length armor of Leonidas, whose statue, on a high pedestal, is in the midst of the town of Sparta, should you ever get that way.

Guicciardini, the great Florentine historian, alive at the time, had this to say about Julius: "He was a soldier in a cassock; he drank and swore heavily as he led his troops; he was willful, coarse, bad-tempered and difficult to manage. He would ride his horse up the Lateran stairs to his papal bedroom and tether it at the door." And he loved being called the Warrior Pope.

Peter O'Toole portrayed him perfectly in the series *The Tudors*, both his character and physically, but only at the very end of his life did he resemble the painting by Raphael where he comes through weak and sickly, inappropriate for a man who had led armies and reigned supreme over European diplomacy. His life was largely covered in Part II, but some details and anecdotes need be furnished. For example, Raphael shows him wearing a beard, a practice forbidden by canon law, but he only did so for a year as a sign of mourning at the loss of Bologna, a vital Papal State.

Born Giuliano della Rovere (we'll call him della Rovere until he becomes pope), he may have been both the son *and* lover of Sixtus IV, an accusation made also concerning Alexander VI and *his* bastard son Cesare (several sources, existent at the time, maintain that this was so, but then Julius and Sixtus, Alexander and Cesare, had many enemies). He was education among Franciscans by Sixtus himself, and was Sixtus' altar boy when Sixtus became pope. Della Rovere was endowed by the same Sixtus with numerous bishoprics, making him a wealthy young man. He was a papal legate in France for four years, which served him mightily when Alexander became pope and he had to flee to France to escape Alexander's wrath because he had accused him of buying the papal election. He convinced the French king Charles VIII to intervene in Italian affairs by invading Italy, but Alexander, subtle, intelligent and *in power*, outmatched della Rovere who had to wait for Alexander's death to have a try at the Vatican, but another was elected, Pope Puis III, who luckily had only 26 days to live. In the meantime della Rovere gained Cesare's support due to Cesare's illness which nearly finished him off, and due to della Rovere's promise to reinstate Cesare as head of papal troops and assure him that he would retain all of the land he had conquered under his father Alexander. Cesare was no fool except this one time. He gave his support to della Rovere who was unanimously elected pope except for two votes, della Rovere's own and the French Cardinal d'Amboise who wanted the job for the glory of France (receiving della Rovere's vote, out of friendship, in the attempt). Naturally, the usual bribes--money and a mightier position in the food chain--won the day. Cesare was killed, as related earlier, and Julius II erased every remaining trace of Alexander. As Nigel Cawthorne wrote, ''I will not live in the same rooms as the Borgias. Alexander desecrated the Holy Church as none before. He usurped the papal power by the devil's aid, and I forbid under the pain of excommunication anyone to speak or think of Borgia again. His name and memory must be forgotten. It must be crossed out of every document and memorial. His reign must be obliterated. All paintings made of the Borgias or for them must be covered over with black crepe. All the tombs of the Borgias must be opened and their bodies sent back to where they belong—to Spain.'' The Borgia apartments would remain sealed for over 300 years!

One of the major problems for the new pope was Henry VIII who wanted a divorce. A papal dispensation had already allowed Henry to marry Catherine of Aragon who had been Henry's brother's bride for six months before he died, leaving Catherine a virgin as he had been to ill to be operative—although the day after the wedding he bragged to his friends, ''Last night I visited the depths of Spain.'' The refusal to allow the divorce would end Catholicism in England, all because the king wanted to fuck his way through seven additional wives.''

The second problem was the Papal States, governed by lords, dukes, princes, et al. that the pope wanted returned to the bosom of the church. In a series of wars far too complicated and ephemeral to discuss here--the War of the Holy League, the Italian Wars, the Battle of Agnadello, the War of the League of Cambrai, among others--he simply died too soon to succeed, of fever, and with him his dream of a united Italy died too.

He had put Michelangelo to the task of constructing his tomb, commissioned in 1505 and finished in 1545. It was originally intended for St. Peter's Basilica but wound up in the church of San Pietro in Vincoli. Although the actual tomb is colossal, with 7 statues, including the magnificent Moses, the original would have been far bigger, comprising 40 statues, some of the unfinished ones now on view in the Louvre. Only the Moses has a commanding presence and an anecdote has it that it was so lifelike that when finished Michelangelo struck it on the knee with a hammer, saying ''NOW SPEAK!'' The hammer mark can be seen today. As for Julius, he was buried far from his monument, in St. Peter's Basilica.

Michelangelo had also been appointed to paint the Sistine Chapel, named after Sixtus IV who restored it. Julius was said to have appreciated the physical beauties of the men painted by Michelangelo but part of their beauty was destroyed forever when one of Michelangelo's associates, Daniele da Volterra, was ordered to cover up the genitals following the genius' death. But he didn't touch the acorns and oak leaves present, the first representing the male glans and the second the renewal of sexuality, among other things. The central *Creation of Adam* is certainly the most stirring work of art known to humanity.

One of Julius' lovers is thought to be Giovanni Alidosi who accompanied della Rovere to France. Julius made him a cardinal and he served as an intermediary between the pope and Michelangelo, as both were headstrong and difficult (just the negotiations concerning the Sistine Chapel, before a single brush stroke, took two years!). As mentioned above, Julius lost Bologna and as a consequence Alidosi had three persons found guilty of aiding both the Bolognese and the Venetians. They were strangled to death under his orders. Of Alidosi, Cardinal Bembo said, ''Faith meant nothing to him, nor religion, nor trustworthiness, nor shame, nor anything that was holy.'' Much hated, Alidosi was often caught and tried by various rulers, notably those of Bologna and Urbino, ruled by the pope's nephew, Francesco Maria della Rovere, but instead of dispatching the reviled cardinal he was always given a trial, time enough for Julius to intervene in his favor. As Francesco had been appointed general to conquer Bologna and had failed to do so, he was summoned to Rome to explain himself to his uncle the pope. After the meeting, while heading back to his lodgings on horseback, accompanied by a group of his soldiers, he crossed the path of Alidosi who was on his way to dine with the pope. Alidosi saluted Francesco in an arrogant way that displeased one of Francesco's followers, just a youngster, who dismounted and knifed Alidosi, sitting on his mule, in the throat. From then on it was an eating-frenzy of boys out to kill each other.

Francesco's men won out, and while Alidosi's went scurrying away, Francesco's took turns slicing off pieces of Alidosi's face and plunging daggers into his body. Julius had the pieces interred and realpolitik obliging, suffered his pain in private.

Another lover was supposedly Luigi Pulci, a poet described by Cellini as being beautiful and talented. The Venetian diarist Girolamo Priuli maintains that Julius brought to Rome "some very handsome young men with whom he was publicly rumored to have sex, and he was said to be the passive partner." When attacking Bologna a sonnet circulated, advising Julius to return to Rome where he could content himself with "Squarcia and Curzio in your holy palace/keeping the bottle in your mouth and a cock up your ass." It *was* true that he drank a lot.

Julius made plans to demolish the old basilica of St. Peter's and replace it with a huge basilica, the whole serving to house Julius' final resting place, the greatest tomb ever erected. Michelangelo was chosen to design it as well as to build the basilica, but over the next 120 years the combined efforts of popes and architects were needed to see it through. It is believed that St. Peter was crucified there, at the emplacement of the current obelisk, by Nero who held the Christians responsible for the burning of the city. As for Julius, Michelangelo finally finished his tomb after 40 years of bargaining and labor. Julius wasn't interred there though. For all his efforts he was accorded a simple slab of marble on the floor of the basilica, that people walk over every day, knowing little of the headstrong warrior beneath.

PART V

MICHELANGELO
1475 - 1564

Few men had lived a longer, fuller life than Michelangelo, perhaps none had bequeathed as much artistic wealth to humanity as this tortured genius, dead at age 89. The body was destined for burial in the Basilica of St. Peter's still under construction, but was stolen by Florentines in the midst of the night, destination a city Michelangelo had not visited for 30 years, his nonetheless beloved Florence. Paraded through the streets to his last resting place, word of mouth spread as to who it was, and soon the streets were jammed with crowds. At the Basilica of Santa Croce the coffin was opened for the benefit of the crowd. The body within was intact, clean and totally lifelike a month after his passing, proof to the assembled masses of the artist's sanctity. But he had not had the luck of going to his tomb in company of his lover, as did Caravaggio with Cecco and da Vinci with Salaì and Melzi. The love of Michelangelo's deams, Tommasso, was absent, and the love of his life, Urbino, had preceded him in death.

Michelangelo was born a Florentine and he died a Florentine, even if his birth had taken place outside of Florence in Caprese, and he had been destined for burial in Rome. The Florence of that epoch was the most beautiful city in the world, 30,000 Florentines massed together between walls that surrounded the town, a space so narrow it could be walked across in an hour. Divided in half by the Arno where ruddy-cheeked boys swam naked in its refreshing waters, Florence was the birthplace of the Renaissance and home to the hallowed sextet, da Vinci, Michelangelo, Raphael, Botticelli, Cosimo and his grandson Lorenzo *Il Magnifico*.

His full name was Michelangelo di Lodovico Buonarroti Simoni, his father was Lodovico who was forced to place him in the bustling workshop of the immense painter Ghirlandaio, at age 10. Forced because the lad was headstrong despite, says Ascanio Condivi, a painter and Michelangelo's biographer, Lodovico's ''outrageously beating him.'' Lodovico had destined the boy for more literary quests, beginning with the obligatory study of Latin, a language Michelangelo would always regret not having learned as it separated him from the ranks of the nobility he admired, a regret that burned like a coal until the day he died. But he did make it to Ghirlandaio's, as if directed by the hand of God, as Leonardo had been fortunate in finding Verrocchio. Michelangelo's older brother, Lionardo, didn't fare as well. Destined for commerce, his father placed him with an abacus teacher, obligatory for the times, Raffaello Canacci, who sodomized the boy, age 10, ''often and often from behind,'' he admitted to the court. He was fined 20 florins and a year in prison which was dropped because he confessed his sin. Lionardo entered the orders, became a Dominican friar, and disappeared from history. Lodovico had five sons about whom he said, ''None of them would give me the slightest help or even a glass of water.'' If one son was beaten and another raped—and God knows what happened to the other three boys—then it stands to reason that they would flee their father's care and not look back. But we do know that only one son married.

Michelangelo learned about Ghirlandaio's workshop thanks to a boy two years older, Francesco Granacci, who would remain his friend until his death. Together they were sent to work for Lorenzo *Il Magnifico* who owed a part of his prestige to his position as patron of the arts. At the moment Lorenzo lacked sculptors and Ghirlandaio sent him the two promising boys. Here Condivi recounts the charming story of Lorenzo coming on Michelangelo as he was sculpting a faun. He pointed out to the boy, then 15, that a faun as old as the one his was creating wouldn't have had a mouth of such perfect teeth. Michelangelo is said to have not been able to hold still until Lorenzo had left so he could knock out a tooth, and then he couldn't wait until Lorenzo returned and admired what he had done. Alas for boy and man, Lorenzo, although still young, had but four years left to live. About Lorenzo the great historian Guicciardini wrote, "No one, not even his enemies, denies that he was a very great and extraordinary genius." Lorenzo provided him and Granacci a room and a place at his excellent and refined table. Yet despite the refinement, Lorenzo's household was run on an extremely informal basis. One was free to come and go as one wished, and to say what one wished, and Lorenzo himself was always available to boys like Michelangelo, whereas visitors of high rank often had to cool their heels for days before being admitted into his presence. A grown man was present, Poliziano, a professor and Latin poet, a founder of humanism. He translated works from the Greek, especially Plutarch and Plato. He was also a rampant lover of boys, and one can only wonder what effect his intelligence and enticing talk had on seducing the young artist, if any. He took an interest in Michelangelo and was said "to have loved him greatly." Francesco Granacci, on the other hand, would have made a perfect first friend for Michelangelo (he is painted in the nude in the painting *The Raising of the Son of Theophilus* by Filippino Lippi). Another boy was also present, Pietro Torrigiano whom I mentioned in Part II. He too was a sculptor under Lorenzo's patronage, and later he brought the artistic segment of the Renaissance to England where he finished his life. He was also an insufferable bully and when Michelangelo made some disparaging remark concerning his work, he broke the artist's nose, an infliction that greatly diminished Michelangelo's faith in himself, as he felt he was no longer handsome. (Some say he was Michelangelo's boyfriend and the dispute was in reality a quarrel between lovers.) Afraid of Lorenzo's reaction, Torrigiano fled to Cesare Borgia who was offering money to enroll new army conscripts, and as Torrigiano needed money and was physically fearless, he joined his troops. Afterwards, as I've said, he went to England where his destiny was fulfilled.

Having his nose broken was the beginning of a series of ordeals for the young Michelangelo. Lorenzo *Il Magnifico* died at age 43, certainly from problems centered around the family plague, gout. How this singular light in the history of humanity, ruler of Florence since the age of 20, so strong, courageous and vibrant could just cease to exist was incomprehensible. An event of far less importance, but one that was nonetheless destabilizing, was a charge by a youth called Mancino that Poliziano had repeatedly sodomized him. There followed a roundup in the taverns of anyone in the company of boys. Michael Rocke, in his wonderful *Forbidden Friendships*, points out that by age 30 one out of every two youths in Florence had been arrested for sodomy; by age 40 two out of every three men had been incriminated. As these acts took place in private, and were therefore rarely discovered, it meant that literally every boy, youth and man was doing it. When the dust following Poliziano's arrest settled, those found guilty were fined and they all went right back to satisfying their loins. Priests ardently preached against sodomy, their eyes bulging with hatred for the vile act, spewing saliva over the faithful in their haste to denounce it, while below the pulpit the choir and altar boys quietly awaited the private behind-doors ceremony to follow, when the priests, aroused by the heat of their sermons, would savagely penetrate one of the less fortunate among them. It took place then as it takes place now, and we continue, like them, to do absolutely nothing.

Lorenzo's son Piero had a footman who ran alongside him as he rode, acting both as groom and bodyguard. Piero described the man as exceptional in his beauty and perfect in body. Michelangelo drew the man, as he did others of great beauty and physical perfection who worked for the Medici. In the closed circle of the Medici, which counted palazzos and villas the size of mansions, immense parks consisting of rivers and lakes, of artists, tutors and in-house philosophers convinced of the singular majesty found in the male body, boys and men were plentiful, available, from laborers to grooms to models and apprentices, most of whom were open to the intimacy that allowed the Medici and their guests, Michelangelo included, a chance to familiarize themselves—during languorous Medici nights—with a male's attributes, his nipples, navel, veins, pubic bush, testicles and foreskin, knowledge of which Michelangelo would need to perfect his future *David*.

Now comes a strange interlude in Michelangelo's life. In Part II we learned that Charles VIII invaded Italy and appropriated Florence, to the humiliation of Piero de' Medici who tried to deal with Charles but was turned away like a servant. He fled Florence and entered history as Piero the Unfortunate. In fear of Charles' army, Michelangelo escaped to Bologna where he and two friends who accompanied him were jailed because they didn't have the small sum of money needed to buy permission to stay in the city, an important source of taxes for towns like Bologna, one that permitted them to do things like medical dissections which, in Bologna, had been carried out in public for centuries. Somehow an important Bolognese personage recognized him as a Medici sculptor from Florence and paid for his release, taking the boy to his palazzo. Now, Michelangelo would be remembered throughout history as being tight-fisted in the extreme, rarely inviting friends to share a meal, and he never accepted gifts for fear of being placed in a person's debt. But he was also generous to those he loved, literally giving them the shirt off his back. The paradox is that Michelangelo rarely went through life with the same people, no matter how much he had loved them in the past. Only when he was in the throes of love was he fierce and total. Da Vinci, on the other hand, kept loyal to friends and remained close to his lovers until the end, but in a way that may have been too cerebral in comparison to Michelangelo, who loved his boys fully and violently. Be that as it may, Michelangelo was said to have abandoned his two friends in prison and went off to live in such luxury that when Piero de' Medici happened to come to Bologna, Michelangelo didn't even make an effort to see him.

He and his new friend, Gian Francesco Aldrovandi, spent their nights reading Boccaccio, literature as erotic then as it is to us today. A friendship developed ... and perhaps more. At any rate Michelangelo carved three small statues for Aldrovandi's church, St Dominic, each around 2 feet high, of extreme beauty and intricacy, especially the angel (details of which are on the Net). After a year Michelangelo returned to Florence where the political situation had stabilized, and then went to Rome where he sculpted the *Pietà*, Christ cradled on the legs of his mother, whose portrait is so young she could have been Christ's sister. Michelangelo inscribed his name on a band across her breasts, the first and only time he ever signed a work. The perfection of the faces and the intricacy of Christ's mother's drapery are beyond human understanding as to how Michelangelo accomplished it. He was 25, the new and never to be toppled King of the World.

David was next, carved from a block of Carrara marble that had been awaiting the genius, in Florence, for 40 years. Since his early teens Michelangelo had dissected bodies, learning the secrets of tissue, muscles, veins, skin and bone, a grisly, horrifying experience in times without the least refrigeration, a task he's said to have enjoyed, certainly in the sense of a stepping stone to what would become, at age 26, his and the world's foremost masterpiece. *David* that would reign until the end of time as the measure of perfect manhood. A distant secondary miracle, but a miracle just the same, was the consent of the population to dissections, which had taken place in Bologna, as I've said, since the early 1300s. Dissections were anathema under the Romans and the Arabs who, even so, had been known for their advances in medicine.

A month after he started *David* he requested that a wall be built, allowing him to continue in private. Nearly two years later, it was removed. The problem arose as to where to put it. So great was its immediate impact that a panel of Italy's finest artists and most prominent citizens, 28 in number, including Botticelli, Filippino Lipp, Piero di Cosimo and da Vince himself, were united to decide where to put it. Months of discussion ended in accepting Michelangelo's own request to place it in the Piazza della Signoria. It was pulled there over greased wooden beams. It was positioned on a plinth and its genitals covered with a garland, and there it would remain until eventually placed in the Accademia di Belle Arti in 1873.

The first miracle was its creation, the second its perfection thanks to the acceptance of dissection, and the third is that it has gone through riots, revolutions and wars and has come out unscathed, although nearly immediately four louts were imprisoned for throwing stones at it, perhaps jealous of its virility, and had to pay heavy fines. Vasari wrote that once one had seen *David*, one need never look at another statue. Strangely, at that very time another statue came to light, one sculpted well before the birth of Christ, unearthed in a field outside Rome in the presence of Michelangelo himself who had been summoned to see it. It is now in the Vatican and is proof that other magnificent creations *are* still worth seeing. It is the *Laocoön*, the story of which can be found in my book *TROY*. What Vasari perhaps meant, and what is the truth, is that *David* is the greatest sculpture in existence.

After the *Pietà* Michelangelo did another virgin and child, the *Bruges Madonna*, for a Bruges merchant, and then the *Pitti Tondo,* a virgin and child carved from marble in the form of a sphere, not unlike a bas-relief. Martin Gayford in his wonderful *Michelangelo* (see Sources at end of book) claims that the model for this was a man. The chisel strokes are highly visible, supposedly because Michelangelo liked this particular carving in this unpolished fashion.

Julius II became pope, taking Julius Caesar's first name as his own. Julius asked Michelangelo to build his tomb and asked where it should be placed. Michelangelo answered "in St. Peter's that I will build." "At what cost," asked the pope. "100,000 ducats" was the artist's answer. "Make it 200,000" was Julius' rejoinder.

He went to Carrara to command the marble. Martin Gayford takes over with this amazing scene: "One day when he was high up in the mountains above the town of Carrara, looking down at the peaks and valleys below and the Mediterranean in the distance beyond, he formed the wish to make a colossus that would be visible to mariners from afar. In other words, Michelangelo wanted to carve a chunk of mountain into a human figure. One guesses, though the subject is not described, that he had in mind a naked male body."

Julius was as impossibly irascible as was Michelangelo. When the artist went to see him and was repeatedly turned away, Michelangelo left for Florence. The pope, furious, sent five horsemen to bring him back, but as Florence was beyond the church's pale, they could do nothing. Political infighting ensued between the pope and Florence, the end result being that Michelangelo was forced to capitulate as no one could conceive of defying the pope. Then, as would happen again and again, the pope changed his mind, deciding that painting the upper reaches of the Sixteen Chapel should come first. He rode off to war with Bologna and, winning, then decided that a statue of himself should mark the event. Michelangelo was called for and actually did cast a huge figure in honor of Julius, a statue that was melted down the moment Bologna was lost. And Gayford writes: "The tantalizing suspicion is that it must have been a masterpiece."

Michelangelo returned to Rome and started work on the Sistine Chapel, painted daily on fresh plaster, a technique of such huge difficulty that even da Vinci is suspected of having given up work on his *Battle of Anghiari* because of his failure in mixing the right components, and then, later, making mistakes when doing *The Last Supper* which, consequently, is lost to us forever. That Michelangelo succeeded on just the mechanics, mechanics on such an incredible scale, is in itself a miracle, not counting, afterwards, the choice of the right oils and right pigments. A patch of plaster to be covered during a day's work was called a *giornata*, the seams of which cannot be seen from afar. Errors could be made up for by painting over the dried plaster, *a secco*. The Sistine paintings are a homage to the male body. In the part dedicated to the story of Noah, called *The Drunkenness of Noah*, Gayford points out that not only was Noah painted in the nude, his sons, shown covering the body while averting their eyes, were also painted—for absolutely no biblical reason—stark naked too. Gayford adds an interesting insight into why the church allowed nudity, saying that it was acceptable because God had made Christ as an incarnation of man, and so the body was not a shameful object. ''Here was a theological reason to decorate the chapel with buttocks, penises, biceps and pectorals.'' Four years later, at the end of his labors, Michelangelo wrote in a letter to his father, ''I work harder than anyone who has ever lived!''

In Part II we learned that Lorenzo *Il Magnifico* had his son Giovanni named a cardinal at the ripe old age of 13. He was now 37 and pope, taking the name Leo X, although his coronation had to be put off until he was consecrated a priest, which had not as yet been the case. He is shown, fat, in a painting by Raphael, *Portrait of Leo X*, alongside his handsome brother, Cardinal Giulio di Guiliano de' Medici, son of *Il Magnifico's* assassinated brother, and future Pope Clement VII. Leo X was notorious for both the selling of indulgences and his homosexuality, of which there is no detailed confirmation. Along the same lines, Leo summoned Raphael to adorn the Vatican sauna with erotic paintings, in a room called the Stufetta del cardinal Bibbiena, one of which shows the randy goat-god Pan leaping from the bushes with a monstrous erection.

On the sexual front Michelangelo could solicit whom he wished, although longer, more intense relations were known to have existed with Piero d'Argenta, an assistant, and an assistant known as Silvio, whose bedside he refused to leave when the boy became ill. Antonio Mini, 17, replaced Gherardo Perini, 19, who wrote that he was ready to offer Michelangelo any service. Niccolò da Pescia, ''who lives with me,'' wrote the master, followed. There was Febo di Poggio and then Federico Ginori that Cellini describes as a young man with a fine spirit, noble, with handsome looks, whom a princess later took for lover.

We need now interrupt our story with an interlude to catch up on the political situation throughout Italy. Part II ended with the death of Alexander VI, a saint or scumbag according to whom one reads, and his son Casare, handsome, fearless, virile, a magnet to those like me who try to flush out the rare and unexpected (the key being, as Diaghilev said, *"Étonne-moi!"*), but no less reprehensible than his father the pope. These were extraordinary times, and what follows now is no less so, for we are discussing Italy and the Renaissance, a time as hallowed as Ancient Greece and Ancient Rome. In a word, we're talking about the very center of the world.

For me the Renaissance died in 1492 with the loss of Lorenzo *Il Magnifico*, but the death rattle continued on until the passing of Michelangelo. We'll nonetheless make our way to Caravaggio, as no history of sexuality would be complete without this genius, whose boy portraits are so living that one came inhale the lads' pheromones.

After the death of Alexander Julius II decided he would have all the Papal States returned to the church, as a first step in reuniting the whole of Italy under his sagacious direction. Florence was necessary to the pope, but with the passing of Lorenzo Florence was no longer the same. As Vasari said of Botticelli, "Old and useless, ill and decrepit" he hobbled through the streets of Florence on crutches, an incarnation of the city itself. Luca Landucci, an apothecary who kept a diary, thanks to which Luca lives on through history, wrote this: "Three men were caught after murdering a Sienese physician. They were tortured most cruelly with red-hot pincers as they were led to the place of their execution. The people cried out for the executioner to make the pincers red hot, as they wanted them to be tortured without mercy. Young boys stood ready to kill the executioner should he not do his work well. The condemned men shrieked in the most horrible manner until hanged." This was what Florence had been reduced to after the Florentines had gotten rid of the last Medici, Piero, because he had failed in his effort to find peace with Charles VIII (Part II).

Now the Florentines elected an honest, industrious man to succeed him, Piero Soderini, who, with the aid of Niccolò Machiavelli, decided to arm the city by establishing a militia, as well as fortifying the wall that surrounded Florence. The pope, in the meantime, had conquered holdouts in the Papal States, such as Bologna (where Michelangelo was called to craft his statue), Rimini, Faenza and Ravenna. Afterward the pope made an alliance with France and Spain to chase away Venice, and then demanded that Italian cities like Florence unite with him to chase away his former allies, the French and Spanish. The pope demanded help from the Florentines who in no way wanted trouble with either France or Spain. They refused their support. Ten thousand of the pope's troops were slaughtered by the French and Spanish, which sent the Florentines into the streets to celebrate with bonfires and singing. Julius descended on Florence with what remained of his army, among whom was Lorenzo *Il Magnifico*'s second son Giovanni, the future Leo X, already fat and thrilled to be surrounded by virile soldiers who sang bawdy songs and bathed naked. (Piero, his first son, had drowned when a boat capsized two years after his father's death.) The troops made it to Prato, on the way to Florence, where the great historian Guicciardini tells what happened next: "The troops sacked the city, full of avarice, lust and cruelty. Two thousand died fleeing or begging for mercy." The town was literally awash with blood. No one was spared, neither children nor women whose naked bodies were left where they lay, in puddles of gore and semen. Despite Florence's preparations for its own safety, the destruction of Prato sent terror through the hearts of all, including Soderini who escaped dressed as a peasant. Medici supporters took over the town and where, just weeks before fireworks had celebrated Julius' military defeat, now crowds cheered as Giovanni de' Medici, the future Clement VII, entered and reoccupied the Medici palazzo. The reception was wildly happy, but nothing compared to a short time afterwards when Giovanni became Pope Leo X following Julius' passing. Then the crowds went crazy with happiness, there were fireworks and cannons fired from the fortifications. Leo X put the city into the hands of Lorenzo, son of his brother, the drowned Piero. Lorenzo was described as energetic, high-spirited and handsome, perhaps too handsome as he forthwith gave up his soul at age 25 due to syphilis and a wound he had received from an arquebus, an early muzzle-loaded rifle. The number of Medici who died young defies the imagination. Luckily, intercourse during the Renaissance was as easygoing with lasses as with lads, otherwise the Medici would have died out (as a large number of other noble families did).

Florence was then turned over to two louts, bastard sons Ippolito and Alessandro de' Medici, while Leo X died and was replaced by Giulio di Giuliano de' Medici, whose father Giuliano had been assassinated in the Santa Maria del Fiori during the Pazzi Conspiracy (and Lorenzo had escaped—Part II). Giuliano became Clement VII. He was a handsome Medici, described as saturnine, cold, morose, disagreeable and a liar. He had nothing going for him except his ability to govern intelligently. As advisor he took the historian, Francesco Guicciardini who thereby had a bird's eye view of what went on in government (like Hadrian who took the immensely important Suetonius as *his* private secretary). Guicciardini didn't last long, no one could around Clement VII, but this was good news as he retired to his villa and his monumental oeuvre, *Storia d'Italia*.

Speaking of louts, during a skirmish someone threw some stones from the roof of a building hovering over *David*. The masterpiece had its arm broken in two places. But Vasari was there, and he and a friend gathered the pieces and saved them for a later restoration.

Around this time there came to pass what is known in history as the Sack of Rome. The sack was carried out by the mutinous troops of the Holy Roman Emperor Charles V. France, Milan, Venice, Florence and Clement VII joined forces to counterman the growing power of Charles. As far as Clement was concerned, he wanted the papacy to be totally free from Charles V's continual intercessions. Charles' troops were persistently victorious but armies cost enormous funds and Charles was late in payment. The troops were a heteroclite mixture of mercenaries, thieves and deserters, even former soldiers leagued against Charles who now thought the wages would be better under the emperor, although there were also a number of followers of Martin Luther who wished to see the anti-Christ, Clement, at the end of a sword, the ultimate problem solver. Before reaching Rome they destroyed other towns, pillaging, raping and massacring. So inured had they become to blood that even the screams of children and babies left them unmoved. In defense of Rome were an estimated 5,000 militiamen and 500 Swiss Guard, mercenaries so valiant and fearless that the popes had taken them as their personal guards and Michelangelo had dressed them, like a Renaissance Yves St. Laurent. Rome also had artillery that was lacking in the rebellious troops. Cellini was present, and later the artist claimed that it was he himself who fatally shot the leader of the rebels, Charles the Duke of Bourbon, who prided himself on his all-white cloak, a marksman's perfect target. The attack was terrible and the Swiss lived up to their reputation by fighting until all were dispatched, except the forty-two who accompanied the pope to the redoubtable fortification Castel Sant'Angelo.

The city was looted, every church, palace and wealthy home. Even peasants from surrounding villages joined in, so great was their hatred of Clement VII whose armies had pillaged their farms and taken their women to feed their bellies and satisfy their groins. Clement finally gave in and paid a ransom of 400,000 ducati for his life, as well as numerous parts of the Papal States. Venice found the moment propitious to seize surrounding properties. From then on Clement would spend the rest of his life avoiding conflict with Charles V. This also led Clement to refuse to grant a divorce to Henry VIII because his wife, Catherine of Aragon, was Charles' aunt, thus opening the way for the English Reformation and the loss of an entire nation under the Catholic Church, freeing Henry to fuck his way to the summit of history. Rome's population was said to have plummeted from 55,000 before the attack to 10,000 after. Ten thousand people were thought to have been murdered. Thousands more died from disease caused by unburied bodies. The sack continued on for *eight months*, until there was literally no more to steal, no more undiseased women to rape and no more food to eat.

In memory of the valiant Swiss Guard (they may seem tame today, but back then they were the cream of the fighting crop) new guardsmen are now sworn in on the 6th of May, the first day of the Sack of Rome.

It was now that Alessandro de' Medici, age 19, was placed as ruler of Florence by his purported father, none other than Pope Clement VII. He was aided by his cousin Ippolito. Immediately Alessandro ordered the building of a massive fortress whose canons could be swiveled to point to an approaching enemy ... or on Florentines themselves. He impounded weapons in private hands and ordered the bell in the Palazzo della Signoria--the bell that had sounded for centuries, warning the Florentines of danger within or outside of the walls, the bell that had rung when Lorenzo *Il Magnifico* had been attacked and his brother killed, summoning Florentines and farmers alike to protect this great Medici--he ordered it, as I said, to be melted down. Alessandro was hated and his end was incredible, an end that I shall save until the chapter on Cellini who witnessed it all.

Alessandro was replaced by Cosimo de' Medici, only 17. Tall, handsome (his portrait by Jacopo Pontormo shows an exquisite youth) and knowledgeable. His father was Giovanni, the youngest son of Caterina Riario Sforza de' Medici whom we discussed at great length in Part II. He was secretive, cold, insulting and he trusted no one which probably saved his life on several occasions as old Florentine families like the Strozzi and the Salviati tried to overthrow him, only to be beheaded in public. He called upon Cellini on numerous occasions but he soon lost all heart for both art and politics when he lost two sons to malaria. The third son, Francesco, ruled in his place while he lived, and became Duke of Florence after his death. Cosimo died at age 55, young in a sense, but old when compared to other Medici who died much younger. This ends our political interlude.

Michelangelo did an enormous number of statues throughout his life, by my count around 45. Some, like the *Pietà*, *Moses*, the *Rebellious Slave* and, of course, *David*, stir me personally to my innermost soul. He lived 89 years, and as he said himself, it would have taken four lifetimes to accomplish all he wanted to accomplish. But a lot of time had been wasted, nearly *40 years* on just the tomb of Julius II, the finality of which leaves much to be desired. On the other hand, if he had just done *Moses*, only *Moses*, for Julius' tomb, it would be declared, today, a perfect success, one of the wonders of the world. Time wasted haggling over money and details. Time wasted by popes demanding one thing, only to change their minds in favor of something else. Literally years were spent at Carrara seeking out the best marble. One thing is for certain, after his run-in with Julius no other pope ever treated him like a servant again. He sculpted the Tomb of Giuliano de' Medici: Giuliano himself, as well as a male nude (*Day*) and a woman (*Night*) who is nothing more than a male nude with breasts. Then he sculpted the Tomb of Lorenzo di Piero de' Medici showing Lorenzo, a male nude (*Dusk*) and another male nude with breasts (*Dawn*). Michelangelo hadn't tried to make the statue of Giuliano (whom he had known well, Lorenzo too) resemble in any way Giuliano, and the same with Lorenzo. When someone criticized this he answered, Who cares? In a thousand years no one will remember what they looked like. He did another statue, *Victory*, a naked boy with a strangely small head.

Sexually, he had his models and assistants, all of whom happened to be among the most beautiful and desirable boys found wherever he decided to set down roots. Michael Rocke tells us of a letter Machiavelli wrote to a friend, describing, in couched terms, what men did at night in Florence, what Michelangelo certainly did: "A man of my acquaintance went from one site to another that lads are known to frequent, and then wound up finding 'a little thrush' agreeable to being kissed and having 'his tail-feathers ruffled.' After this successful find, the man sealed his conquest," as Machiavelli put it, "by thrusting his *uccello* (dick) into the *carnaiulo* (ass)." Benvenuto Cellini (whose life is coming up) writes, in his autobiography, about a youth called Luigi Pulci "whose singing was so lovely that Michelangelo, that superb sculptor and painter, used to rush along for the pleasure of hearing him whenever he knew where he was performing." Cellini goes on to say that Pulci's father had been beheaded for incest and that the boy had "just left some bishop or other, and was riddled with the French pox." Cellini nursed him back to health, Martin Gayford tells us, after which the boy had an affair with the nephew of a cardinal and with Cellini's own mistress, in revenge for which Cellini wounded him with a sword. Pulci was later killed falling from a horse while showing off in front of Cellini's mistress whom the lad was still seducing. All this is proof again that, in Florence, as in ancient Rome, a boy took advantage of literally any orifice that presented itself. Another source tells us that Michelangelo "spent time without end helping boys, like Andrea Quaratesi, to learn how to draw." As Cicero had said of Plato who insisted he was platonic with boys, "If his aim was only to teach philosophy, how was it that he chose only handsome boys and never ugly ones?" The same was true with Michelangelo. Quaratesi was gorgeous, as seen in the master's drawing of him, *Portrait of Andrea Quaratesi.*

Cellini tells us that despite the revolts and wars and even the plague, Michelangelo had never seemed more relaxed, and indeed took time to wander around the city, paying special attention to handsome young men.

He was nonetheless getting old, around 50, and one wonders what his approach to boys was. Did he feel that his talent and willingness to instruct them compensated for his age, and for his need, ever more desperate, it seemed, as he grew older, to inhale their beauty? Could his art have gone on without them? Could he have survived as an artist for the exclusive sake of art? We won't know because to the very end he remained faithful to both, his art and to the blinding beauty of the boys that inspired it.

As Hadrian had found the boy of his life in Antinous, so too Michelangelo found his in Tommaso Cavalieri, who was described as being of incomparable beauty, of having graceful manners, and '"more to be loved the better he is known." Vasari wrote that he was "infinitely more than any other friend" to Michelangelo. Michelangelo sent him a letter in which he said, "I promise that the love I bear you is equal or perhaps greater to that I ever bore any man, nor have I ever valued a friendship more than I do yours." Thanks to Tommaso Michelangelo would know his own Renaissance, a new life at age 60, and he still had 30 years left to share it with this young gentleman. Michelangelo immediately set himself to drawing, the most rapid way to offer presents. One was *Tityus*. Tityus was Zeus' son who tried to rape Leto, in punishment for which he was eternally attacked by a vulture. Michelangelo showed him, in Gaylord's words, being assaulted with "the great bird's groin pushed against his buttocks." Next came the drawing of *Ganymede*, being carried off to Olympus where he would serve as Zeus' servant and bedmate. Then came *The Risen Christ*, a full-frontal nude, followed by *Phaeton*, the son of Apollo who nagged his father until allowed to drive the chariot of the sun. He lost control and Zeus had to kill him before he hit the earth, destroying it. Another highly unique drawing was *The Dream*, showing a naked young man surrounded by a ring of vices, a woman (a man with breasts) awaiting copulation, the exquisite buttocks of another young man, and a fully engorged dick. The gifts were accompanied by what would turn out to be hundreds of sonnets.

His favorite brother Buonarroto, the only one who married, died, and Michelangelo took over the care of his children, two boys of whom only Lionardo survived, age 9, who came to live with him, and a girl that he put in a nunnery until marriageable age. The story of Lionardo is amusing as later, when he was 20, Michelangelo would fall ill and the boy would rush to his side. But the master knew the boy by then, and knew that only his money interested him. He therefore chased him away, telling him, literally, to never darken his doorway again. But as the lad was the very last of the Buonarroti—and Michelangelo wanted the name to go on—he was forgiven. As I've written, at one time or another Michelangelo broke off with nearly everyone he had known. Even when his brother Buonarroto was living Michelangelo said he was disgusted with his family: "I feel that I no longer have a father or brothers or anyone else in the world."

Michelangelo served the popes in diplomacy. One of his statues, *Heracles*, was sent to François in France, the same François who held the dying head of da Vinci. The artist was also dispatched to Ferrara where the duke, Alfonso d'Este, was wild with joy to receive him. In Part II you may remember my writing this about him: "Alfonso was known to have two interests in life, making cannons in his own personal foundry and parading around town at night, his sword in one hand, his erect cock in the other. His former wife had been so fed up with him that she turned to women for satisfaction. He later married Lucrezia Borgia and at her death he married his mistress, apparently very rare during Renaissance Italy." Due to renewed problems in Florence Michelangelo considered going to the court of François I—he would have been there at the same time as da Vinci—but Florence threatened to jail him if he didn't return home, which he did.

In Florence Michelangelo painted *Leda and the Swan* for his new friend Alfonso d'Este. We see a nude woman in the wings of a swan, its long neck stretched across her belly. You may remember that Zeus took this form to impregnate Leda, slipping his head and neck into her ... well ... you know. The result was that Leda gave birth to twins, Clytaemnestra and Helen, from the same egg, half fertilized by Leda's husband and the other half--the half that produced Helen--by Zeus. (You can find the full story in my book *TROY*.) The painting was later destroyed in France because it was found quasi pornographic.

Clement VII died and Paul III took his place. He had been named a cardinal by Alexander VI because he was the brother of Alexander's mistress. The Romans thereby changed his name from Cardinal Farnese to Cardinal Fregnese, "Cardinal Cunt." Paul III had been waiting years to get his hands of Michelangelo and did so now by ordering him to paint *The Last Judgment* in the Sistine Chapel, an immense work that would require scaffolding seven stories high and take five years to finish, longer than he had taken on the entire ceiling. In other Last Judgments only the damned were featured naked. Here nearly everyone was, the saved and canonized alike. As Gayford says, "nude, curly-haired young men with the bodies of Oympic shot-putters passionately kiss and caress. Some of them hug grey-haired elders." The genitals and asses were later covered with tissue by Michelangelo's assistant, Danielle da Volterra, after his master's death, his only claim to fame. Gayford goes on to give us a quote from Cardinal Tommaso Cajetan that answers the question, What is the difference between being born and being raised? Says Cajetan: " 'What is sown is perishable, what is raised is imperishable. It is sown in dishonor, it is raised in glory. It is sown a physical body, it is raised a spiritual body.' "

Michelangelo received a letter from the playwright and pornographer Pietro Aretino whom we met in the chapter on Raphael. Aretino gave suggestions as to how to paint *The Last Judgment*. Aretino had had to flee Rome after an attempt to assassinate him due to his malicious comments on the clergy. He went to Mantua where its ruler offered to do the job himself in order to gain favor with Rome. Aretino then fled to Venice from whence he wrote Michelangelo. It was a measure of his importance that the artist responded, saying that while the letter filled him with pleasure, it had come too late as he had finished the painting.

To a certain high-ranking critic who was shocked by the nudity in *The*

Last Supper, and suggested that its place was in a sauna or tavern, Michelangelo painted the critic into a corner, showing a serpent chowing down on the critic's penis (find it on the Net because it's hilarious—and magnificent *à la fois*).

Then absolute disaster struck. Francesco d'Amadore, whom he called Urbino, died. He had come into Michelangelo's service as a young man when the master was himself but 30. Michelangelo grew to love Urbino, but in a decidedly different way from Tommaso. Urbino was well cared for, fed and clothed, and he did whatever was needed, from the marketing to the grounding and mixing the paints. But he never received a drawing as did Tommaso. Nor did he merit a sonnet. Yet he was always there. Michelangelo would never put on a clean shirt to greet him, nor, when the sap rose while painting his nudes and he wanted relief, would he need more than pull the ribbons that released the cloth covering his engorged manhood, waiting for Urbino to do the rest. Urbino was always there. Just there. Until he was there no longer. It was then that Michelangelo died, not the biological end that came later. God may not exist but we need Him to exist, He must exist in something, and that something, for Michelangelo, was Tommaso de' Cavalieri. He was the love of Michelangelo's life but not *the* love. That was Urbino, the only person permitted to accompany him during the painting of *The Last Supper*. Just before the end Cellini had pleaded with Michelangelo to return to Florence, leaving Urbino behind to take care of his master's workshop and belongings. As Cellini related in his autobiography, ''Hearing this, Urbino, in an uncouth way, shouted out 'I will never leave Michelangelo, not until either he or I is under the ground'.''

Surrounded by what the world has to offer in supreme beauty, Michelangelo died alone, having pushed away even Tommaso at the end, thusly sparing himself the cruelest of all destinies, seeing his own ugliness reflected in the eyes of those he had cherished most, the eyes of his lovers, models, assistants, apprentices, boys he met and offered to draw or to teach how to draw, boys in taverns and in allies after dark in a city, Florence, reputed for its warm nights of sublime encounters with the imperishable boys of imperishable Italy. There would be no Salaì or Melzi at his side. Like Hadrian who lost Antinous, he too would meet his maker alone--the world's supreme artist, not just in his time, but of all time.

PART VI

VIGNETTES

DONATELLO
1408 – 1466

Donatello's art seduced Cosimo—as his body did many a Florentine male—who put up with his every caprice. When a merchant refused a bronze head that Donatello had spent a month producing, arguing that a month's labor wasn't worth so much, Donatello sent it hurling from the heights of a tower where it had been taken to capture the best light, all the while protesting that he was an artist, not some laborer paid monthly wages. Cosimo then commissioned a bronze statue of *David* from Donatello, a hero prized by Florentines because he had overcome the tyranny of Goliath. The result pleases some; for others it is a girlish body with minimal male equipment. Mary MacCarthy called the androgynous bronze ''a transvestite's and fetishist's dream of alluring ambiguity.'' One can hardly imagine this *David* winning a victory against Mighty Mouse let alone Goliath. Donatello placed his earnings in a basket in his studio and told his assistants to serve themselves with what they needed, but lovers who looked elsewhere were threatened with death by the artist who would run after them wherever they fled, a form of exercise that kept him alive until age eighty. He once requested permission from Cosimo to follow one of his runaway boys to Ferrara where he planned to kill him. Cosimo warned the Count of Ferrara who managed to put the boys together, both of whom immediately broke down with laughter and shared a kiss. One of my sources claims that ''laughter'' in this sense was a *mot à clef* meaning to fuck.

Donato di Niccolò di Betto Bardi was born in Florence and started his early training in a goldsmith's workshop, followed by a stay in the studio of Lorenzo Ghiberti who spent 21 years completing the bronze doors of the Baptistery of Florence Cathedral that Michelangelo called the ''Gates of Paradise.''

POLIZIANO
1454 – 1494
PICO DELLA MIRANDOLA
1463 – 1494

Poliziano, born Angelo Ambrogini in Montepulciano, was a Renaissance humanist philosopher who studied under Ficino at his Platonic Academy and later taught at the University of Florence. His father was a jurist murdered by the enemies of the Medici because he championed their cause. His scholastic preeminence brought him to the attention of the Medici who hired him to tutor their boys, one of whom was Piero who formed a strong bond of friendship with Poliziano.

He was a known lover of boys, some very young, and had been charged by Florentine authorities with sodomy, charges dropped thanks to the influence of his patrons the Medici. They too severed their relations with Poliziano but later reinstated him, leaving one with the impression that he had not been dismissed due to overly affectionate caresses involving Piero and his brothers.

His portrait, accompanied by the child Giuliano de' Medici, can be seen in a fresco painted by Domenico Ghirlandaio in the Sassetti Chapel, Santa Trinita, in Florence. Piero de' Medici, sublimely beautiful, is portrayed in a sumptuous painting by Botticelli in his *Madonna del Magnificat*.

Politiziano may well have been intimate with Medici guests, among whom Michelangelo, Ficino, Donatello and Pico della Mirandola. In 2007 the bodies of della Mirandola and Poliziano were deterred from San Marco in Florence and found to have been poisoned by arsenic.

Politiziano may have known all of the above biblically, but for Pico della Mirandola the love of his life was Girolamo Benivieni who was placed in the same grave as Pico, 49 years after Pico's death, as Girolamo died at age 89! So strong was the love they had shared that Girolamo waited that long to be reunited with his lover.

Pico della Mirandola was a humanist philosopher like Poliziano, familiar with Latin, Greek, Hebrew and Arabic. Somewhat like Plato, he claimed that perfection was found in the virtuous love of a young man, meaning that the older man shared his knowledge with the younger, a virtuous idea indeed. The problem was that they hid the sexual side, pretending that it never existed, but Savonarola, who really knew a lot when it comes down to it, found out, and at Pico's death he told his congregation that Pico was spending some time in purgatory for unspecified sins.

Be that as it may, Pico did die within two months of Poliziano, and although the arsenic found in both is inexplicable, modern historians feel relatively certain they both died of syphilis.

FICINO
1433 – 1499

The problem with men like Ficino wasn't that they were Nioplatonists, but that they pretended to be platonic in their relationships with boys. In the Florence of *Il Magnifico*, where one usually got a slap on the wrist when caught in flagrante delicto but could also, depending on the situation and the man's social status, find himself separated from his head, one was forced to lie. Ficino, like Varchi like Poliziano like so many others, all claimed to inhale boyish aromas from afar—a necessary claim, certainly, but one far, far from the truth. Cellini himself, when accused of sodomy by a jealous artist, in front of Cosimo, maintained the Ganymedism was the realm of the gods, and not for simple artisans like himself, causing Cosimo to break out in laughter, acknowledging that, indeed, such mores were certainly foreign to the likes of the creator of *Perseus*.

As well as being a Nioplatonist—a humanist philosopher—Ficino was also an astrologer. His father was a physician under the patronage of the Medici who took Ficino into their household. Ficino tutored Lorenzo *Il Magnifico* and Giovanni Pico della Mirandola, destined to be another humanist philosopher, who was perhaps his lover (according to several sources). Following in his father's footsteps, Ficino too became a physician, and later a priest.

The love of his life was the young Giovanni Cavalcanti to whom he wrote ardent love letters, letters that began with ''Giovanni my most perfect friend,'' *Giovanni amico mio perfettisimo*. The letters were later published. Ficino and Giovanni wrote together side by side, and lived together in a villa at Careggi. Ficino was placed at the head of the Academy that Cosimo had established for the study of Plato. Ficino had learned Greek in order to study Plato's words, wherein lies his fame. His lover Cavalcanti's best known work is *De Amore*. Ficino was also the first person to invent the term platonic love.

We simply know that he died at age 66.

CORREGGIO
1489 – 1534

My approach to Correggio will differ from that of the others of my vignettes in that I'll be mostly dealing with his works of art and not his life, for the simple reason that we known so little about him. But the incredible sensuality of his paintings suggests that he fully appreciated the eroticism found in both sexes. His portrait is included in the *trompe l'oeil* mural seen in the ceiling of the Gay and Lesbian Center in San Francisco, an allegorical painting of men and women moving from the darkness of ignorance into the light of knowledge.

In *Ganymede Abducted by the Eagle* we have Zeus' bedmate locked in his arms as he flies back to Olympus, the whole of little eroticism. One observer notes the boy's ''radiant buttocks'' and draws our attention to the fact that the eagle is licking the his wrist. During the Spanish Inquisition a wealthy connoisseur, Antonio Pérez, was charged with sodomy, and one of the proofs was his possession of the Ganymede painting. Luckily, Pérez was able to escape to France.

In the painting usually known as *Jupiter and Io*, but also as *Venus and Cupid with a Satyr*, we find Zeus, a wonderfully beautiful naked boy who has taken the form of a satyr, hovering over Aphrodite and a sleeping Eros, with what is surely his engorged maleness hidden by a tissue, the whole wondrously erotic.

We know that Correggio was born Antonio Allegri da Correggio in Correggio, that his father was a merchant whose brother, Lorenzo, was an artist and Correggio's first tutor. Correggio was influenced by da Vinci and Raphael. He spent much of his career in Padua and is thought to have married and engendered at least one son. He was described as being enigmatic in character, melancholic, introverted and "shadowy."

In his *Danaë* we see Zeus in the form of an angel, ready to impregnate the future mother of Perseus (see Cellini). The angel is prepubescent although handsomely muscular.

Two other highly erotic paintings are *Zeus and Io*, Zeus taking the form of a cloud, and *Leda with the Swan,* the swan getting reading to introduce his head and very long neck into the future mother of Helen of Troy (note the athletic youth in the background).

BERNI
1498 – 1535

We've already discussed the destiny of Alessandro de' Medici who was named ruler of Florence after the Sack of Rome by his father Pope Clement VII. Ippolito de' Medici, a cousin, was designated by the same pope to aid Alessandro, but Alessandro, a pleasure-seeking hoodlum whose thrill was freeing girls from their burdensome virginity, especially nuns, and fouling the reputations of virtuous wives, decided to rid himself of Ippolito by ordering Francesco Berni, a highly noted, supposedly extremely funny satirist, to poison Ippolito. When Berni failed to do so, Alessandro had Berni himself poisoned. Berni had found a patron in Ippolito after being dismissed from the service of a distant family relative, Cardinal da Bibiena, for homosexual activity. All of this is covered in obscurity, and some even say that Berni had been ordered to kill someone in the service of Ippolito, and not Ippolito himself. At any rate, 37 is a young age to die.

Berni was noted for his doubles entendres, impossible to translate and understandable only to trained readers, where, as we learn in the *Who's Who in Gay & Lesbian History*, "peaches" meant "cocks." His poetry celebrates physical homosexual encounters.

NICCOLÒ MACHIAVELLI
1469 - 1527

Niccolò Machiavelli served Cesare Borgia, which allowed him an eyewitness view of ruthless government, the foundation of his masterpiece *The Prince*, the very foundation of today's political science. We don't know to what extent he carried on male-to-male relations during his adult life, but thanks to Michael Rocke we have this letter from a childhood friend to Machiavelli who is worried about his son's frequentations, proof of Machiavelli's appreciation of boys during his own adolescence: "Since we are verging on old age, we might be severe and overly scrupulous, and we do not remember what we did as adolescents. So Lodovico has a boy with him, with whom he amuses himself, jests, takes walks, growls in his ear, goes to bed together. What then? Even in these things perhaps there is nothing bad."

Few other times in history were more tumultuous than those known to Machiavelli. Just the mention of names such as the Visconti, the Sforza, the Borgia, Charles VIII and the warrior pope Julius II, brought instant fear to the hearts of men. Battles between the city-states continued without ever a respite. Quarrels between the Medici and their fellow citizens led to the assassination of Lorenzo's brother Giuliano by the Pazzi. Religious unrest caused by the likes of Savonarola, and the miserable decadence of Pope Alexander VI, caused riots and turmoil. Privileged youths such as Cesare and his brothers--and nearly every other boy-delinquent of noble blood-- were free to kill, maim and rape. Condottieri were encouraged to recuperate their wages by destroying villages, towns and cities, and to assuage their lust on girls and women. To these inflictions can be added disease and plague—so terrible that noble families farmed out their children until around age seven, the age at which they were allowed to return home had they survived the various ailments of the times. The peaceable Machiavelli himself was tortured by the usually civilized Medici—with the *strappado*, a torture in five degrees. In the first the prisoner's hands were tired behind his back and he was advised to confess. If he refused, his arms were raised behind his back by a rope attached to a pulley. During this second degree he was lifted off his feet for a short time. If he still refused to confess he faced the third degree, being raised until his arms dislocated. During the fourth degree he was violently jerked. During the last degree, more weights were added until his arms were torn from his body. Machiavelli went as far as the first degree, but as his purported crimes were few, he was let off. He then retired from politics and in a letter to a friend he described a typical day of retirement as one in which he entered his study, wearing the formal dress of an ambassador, and there he discoursed with the popes, princes, kings and emperors of old, asking them questions and noting down their answers.

JULIUS III

1487 - 1555

Julius III was a lucky pope in that during his reign Queen Mary returned to the English throne and Catholicism was restored, all of which led to his glorification and allowed him to live the lazy, dissolute existence he favored. Added to this was the fact that he possessed great administrative talent and as he had been named governor of Rome twice, he had that center too in his corner. He built an incredibly luxurious palace, the Villa Giolia, adorned by the likes of Michelangelo and Vasari and lesser artists who decorated it with Ganymedes and other soft-core pornographic satyrs and naked angels.

Like da Vinci and his Salaì, Julius had fulfilled his erotic fantasies thanks to a youngster, Santino, a streetwise urchin of 14 he saw and lusted for. He had his brother adopt the lad who then became his nephew, on whom he showered benefices and named a cardinal, ennobled under the title of Innocenzo Ciocchi Del Monte. He boasted of the boy's prowess in bed, Julius being the bottom to ''his hung boy.''

Of Julius the governor of Milan wrote, ''They say many bad things about this pope, that he is vicious, arrogant and crazy.'' Thomas Beard wrote: ''He makes a cardinal only of those who bugger him'' The Venetian ambassador to the Vatican, Matteo Dandolo, wrote home to say that ''the pope shared his bed with a boy cardinal.''

After the pope's death Innocenzo killed two men who had insulted him in some unrecorded way. The newly elected Pope Pius IV had him arrested and imprisoned for several years. He was again arraigned for raping two women but was released thanks to Julius' friends. He died in obscurity and was buried, without a funeral, in the Del Monte chapel next to his benefactor who had preceded him in death at age 68, from fever.

SODOMA
1477 – 1549

Il Sodoma was his name and he seemed content to have it. He was extremely prolific, said to base the quality of his painting on the sum of money the patron shelled out. He worked at his own rhythm, when he felt like it, which was nonetheless often. He surrounded himself with a menagerie of animals of every imaginable kind, and boys and young men, boys and young men in profusion, beautiful and all beardless, whom he entertained with jokes and pranks, keeping them in stitches, smiling, always smiling as they horsed around in his bed.

He loved pranks, as I said, and this story has come down to us: A group of monks commissioned a holy scene of virtuous virgins. Sodoma kept the monks out of his studio while he painted a bacchanalia of sluts, the whore friends of his friends. The monks, allowed in, nearly keeled over before the painting, vexed, outraged and determined to destroy it. Sodoma, bent over with peals of laughter, painted draperies over the whores, the end product of which was indeed a scene akin to that of joyous virgins, joyous in their virginal love of Christ.

Sodoma was born Giovanni Antonio Bazzi, son of a shoemaker, in Vercelli but spent the bulk of his life in Siena. He's known to have created scores of paintings, the most famous of which are his *Alexander in the Tent of Darius* and *The Marriage of Alexander and Roxanne*, in which Sodoma highlighted Alexander's lover, Hephaestion, making him naked and accompanied by a boy showing him affection. Sodoma married and had a son, but at the time this was par for the course among ingrain boy lovers. He did a St. Sebastian, beautiful and highly erotic, with a horrifying arrow piercing the youth's neck.

His favorite pastime was the races, in which he entered horses, usually borrowed from patrons. He was well known to the stable boys whom he affected, and his generosity went a long way in winner their affection in return. In circles of debauch he was called only Sodoma, the usage of which one and all found amusing. There is this story told of him: At the end of a certain race the horse he had entered won. The presiding officials asked whose name to call out, as it was the custom to honor the owner in this manner. The stable boys, knowing only that he was called Sodoma, gave that name. The officials just repeated it, paying no attention to its meaning. But the crowds of race goers, mostly old and conservative, raised a howl of protest and Sodoma barely escaped with his life, so bent were they on stoning him to death. He nonetheless recuperated his trophy which he proudly showed visitors to his home from then on.

He died at age 75, eclipsed by the giants, da Vinci, Michelangelo and Raphael. Some say he died unknown and in poverty. But maybe, just maybe, there was a Salaì or a Melzi somewhere in the shadows.

VARCHI
1502 – 1565

Varchi is known as a Neoplatonic humanist, the last of the writers who dared praise male-to-male bonds, just before the descent of the lead curtain lowered by the Tartuffes of the Counterreformation, a movement that was already underway at the end of Ancient Rome, where Hadrian was the last of the emperors to impose his boy, Antinous, on a society gradually slipping away from the freedom of thought and action inspired by the Golden Age of Greece, into the sexual obscurantism that we find to this very day.

Born in Florence, son of a notary, he followed in his father's steps until he decided to devote his time to study and the teaching of literature. One of his lovers was Giovanni de' Pazzi whose uncle Antonio de' Pazzi locked him in his room to prevent the boy from seeing Varchi, but was then caught descending a rope to meet Varchi in the street. Antonio ran after Varchi, knifing him, although not fatally. Varchi then set his sights on Giulianino Gondi whom he loved and then lost when the boy was killed in a street fight. Gondi was succeeded by Lorenzo Lenzi and Giulio della Stufa. Varchi then fell in love with Lorenzo Lenzi, age 10, and had a portrait of the boy painted by Bronzino when Lorenzo was 12. In Padua he was beaten by Piero Strozzi's men when he was found having sex with Piero's younger brother Giulio Strozzi, Varchi's student. There followed inflamed letters to Cesare Ercolani and another 10-year-old, Palla de' Ruccelai, whom he called Cirillo in his writings. And many, many other boys took the places of these.

Varchi's *Storia fiorentina* in 16 volumes was by then so controversial that it was not printed until 100 years later, after all those whose lives he evoked were long dead. Cosimo I had invited him to write the book despite the fact that Varchi had eminently Republican ideals, and Cosimo was just as eminently conservative. The truth concerning certain events, like the death of Alessandro and the intimate contents of letters between men in power and their boys, made *Storia* too hot to touch.

Of Varchi a critic wrote, ''Oh Varchi, our new Socrates, you who prefer young and handsome students, Bembo is waiting for you in the Elysian Fields, his trousers down.'' (Bembo, lover of both Caterina Riario Sforza de' Medici and Lucrezia Borgia swung, like most Florentines, from both sides of the home plate.) Another critic wrote that Varchi would have had more influence in Florence had he ''been less inclined to boy love.'' Indeed, in 1545 he was arrested for sodomy and released only thanks to the intervention of Cosimo, although other sources say he had raped a very young girl, not a boy.

Due to his sonnets that vaunted the glory of male friendships, due to his arrest, he chucked away his humanist ideals and entered the orders, becoming a priest. Unlike Lucrezia Borgia who relished her sexual freedom until her death, Varchi followed in the path of Caterina Riario Sforze de' Medici who had ''known'' some of the worlds most beautiful lads, and had married three, yet she ended up in a nunnery, wedded to Christ.

PART VII

CELLINI
1500 - 1571

What I have to tell you about Cellini reminds me of Carter's discovery of Tutankhamen's Tomb: ''What do you see, Carter?''
''Marvelous things!''
That was Cellini's life, one marvelous discovery after another. He was a rogue, so full of himself that he wrote his autobiography in which he

dared tell all, or nearly all, and what didn't come right out with--his male love affairs for example--he presented in terms that left no possible doubt. Yet no matter how big he tried to make himself in his writings, he would nonetheless never foresee the glory that would be his in the eyes of future generations. He loved life to such an extent that he would never, ever put himself under another's thumb. In Rome as a lad, earning money on the celebrated salt-cellar he carved, he left the workshop where he had learned the trade and went off to study at another. When the owner of the first insisted that he return, Cellini told him outright, I'm a free man and I'll go where I will. When the man insisted more strongly, Cellini put his hand on his sword, making his intentions clear should the affair go farther. He wielded a sword as well as he did a flute, the instrument his father imposed on him as a child of four, one he grew to love but even at that age he knew he would be an artist, and he told his father so. His father. He loved the man and the man loved his boy with every fiber of his soul. When Cellini went off, they both had tears in their eyes. When he returned, they both wept with joy. In the same way Cellini loved his lovers, boys and men to whom he was fiercely loyal. When he returned to Florence from his first adventures, he came across a former friend who greeted him with kisses and an open bed, and when Cellini went off again, the boy plucked a few nascent whiskers for Cellini's chin to keep in memory. And that would continue until his death, many very full years later, at 71. His remains would then be paraded through the streets of his beloved Florence, applauded by dense crowds of admirers, as Michelangelo's had been just seven years before. With women he had children, with his male lovers he was infinitely more tender and affectionate. He continued the tradition that had come down through antiquity, from Gilgamesh and Enkidu, from Patroclus and Achilles, from Alexander and Hephaestion, from Hadrian and Antinous, from David and Jonathan, and from countless, countless others. Cellini's art was all to him, but his boys were more still. They were both the keystone and cornerstone of his existence. And that is as it should be in a life well lived.

Like his many boys, I too love Cellini because he loved life, used life and abused life, and, as important, he allowed life to use and abuse him. He was banished from Florence at age 16, condemned to death at 23, became a soldier at 27, killed a man at 30, and that was just for starters.

But let's go back to the beginning, and in the beginning was a father, Giovanni, who had to wait 18 long years before the woman he loved brought forth a son, whom they welcomed with sobs, litteraly wailing *Sia il benvenuto*! from whence they took his name, Benvenuto. Giovanni marked him out to be a musician and while Cellini practiced day after day Giovanni taught him the rudiments of reading and writing, and a little Greek and Roman mythology. When the child finally made it clear that he would be an artist, Giovanni placed him in the workshop of Michelangelo de' Brandini, but quickly took him out, saying he couldn't live without his boy by his side, although Derek Parker is his excellent *Cellini* thinks it may have been due to the reputation of artists' workshops, where sex between the master, the apprentices and the models was daily routine. Parker points out, as I have through this entire book, that these kinds of relationships were totally par for the course, totally accepted by parents and society, the only way boys could learn about life as girls were shut away. Some workshops, however, gained reputations as nothing more than whorehouses where one could go for sex as one could at any tavern that had rooms. Unhappy with being withdrawn from the workshop, Cellini ran away to Siena where he met a goldsmith, Francesco Castoro who took him in but nevertheless notified Giovanni who came for him. Castoro would play a role in the lad's life later on, a highly positive one. At age 15 Cellini finally gained his freedom to enter the workshop of Antonio di Sandro di Paolo Giamberti, happily known as simply Marcone. He learned to draw and make objects of gold and silver.

Boys loved to dress beautifully, and it was here that the likes of Cellini aided in carving magnificent belt buckles, buttons and brooches of silver. Cesare Borgia, for example, dressed in black, a black cloak fastened with a carved brooch, over a doublet, a snug-fitting buttoned jacket, the buttons also of carved silver, worn over a shirt of cotton, a rare material at that period and so highly prized. The doublet descended to the waist and often had an inner covering of satin, perhaps red. Belts were worn, with at times very large and very beautifully sculpted buckles. Cesare's brother Juan was even more wonderfully dressed. Tight trousers, mostly black, and a doublet closed in front by latches, and slit at the shoulder so that the material of the shirt, usually white, could be seen, contrasting beautifully with the black velvet doublet. The trousers could be of velvet or leather, the genitals covered with drop fronts—cloth attached by ribbons, but the fronts could also be of leather. Codpieces were worn, more and more padded as time passed, emphasizing the wonders they concealed, sticking out over the groin.

By the age of 16 Cellini knew how to protect himself with sword and dagger, as did his younger brother Cecchino. You may remember that I wrote that at that time in Florence a fight could begin if a boy looked at another a nanosecond too long. For some reason known only to boys, Cecchino got into a brawl at age 14 and Cellini came to his aid. Swords were pulled but luckily the neighbors called soldiers who took the boys to court. As boys 13 and over were considered as adults, they could have been severely punished. Due to the daily violence in Florence punishment was harsh in an attempt to keep it down. In the boys' case, they got off easily, with an order to banish them for a period of six months. They went off to

Siena where Castoro, with Giovanni's permission, took them in. Cellini worked on jewelry while Cecchino wandered around the town whiling away time until his father, who wanted him to become a lawyer, would agree to his being a soldier. Giovanni went to Cardinal Giulio de' Medici, the future Clement VII, to plead for his two sons. It was decided that Cellini would go to Bologna to learn music. He did go to Bologna, but to the workshop of Scipione Cavalette where he learned portraiture and design. The boy had it easy wherever he went because he was an easy boy to get to know, charming, talented and certainly charismatic.

He returned to Florence, to his father's arms and a tearful reception, and then to Marcone's studio for more instruction. Here he made the acquantance of someone we've met before, Piero Torrigiani. You may remember that it was he who got into a fight with Michelangelo and broke his nose. He then fled from Florence, joined Cesare Borgia's army and ended up in London where he literally brought the Italian Renaissance. Now he was back in Florence looking for gold workers and he wanted Cellini who was thrilled to be off for England until Torrigiani bragged about having broken the great artist's nose. As Michelangelo was Cellini's hero, Torrigiani was sent packing.

Cellini's sexual life had already begun, but at age 17 he met his first real lover, Giovanni Francesco Lippi, also 17, grandson of the artist Filippo Lippi. About Giovanni Lippi he wrote in his autobiography, ''We were never apart, day and night, and went about together for two years.'' Two years later Cellini had another lover, Giambattista Tasso, a woodcarver, and one day during a stroll … but let Derek Parker tell the story: ''By this time they had reached the San Piero Gattolini gate—the gate by which one leaves Florence to travel towards the Holy City. They looked at each other, threw their aprons over their shoulders, and set off along the road.'' It could have been the Yellow Brick Road, for it led to a long life of adventure.

In Rome Cellini went to work for the goldsmith Firenzuola where he made his superb saltcellar with exquisite miniature masks. He sold it and made off to new adventures elsewhere. Firenzuola didn't see things that way, as he had spent time and money teaching Cellini his trade, but Cellini brushed him off with ''As a free man I'll go when and where I please.'' When Firenzuola lost his temper, Cellini put his hand on the hilt of his sword. Luckily a passerby known to both men stopped to find out what was going on. He got both talking, and in the end Cellini became godfather to one of Firenzuola's children.

He returned to Florence where, at age 23, he and a friend were tried for sodomizing a boy, but as a first offense, they had only to pay 12 bushels of flour each to a local Franciscan convent. As I've stated elsewhere, as sodomy is inherently a private affair, in order for thousands to be caught it had to have been practiced on a huge scale. The known places were the Old

Market, the public baths at San Michele Berteldi and taverns, the most notorious of which was the Buco, meaning anus, off the via Lambertisca near the Ponte Vecchio, where one could drink before retiring to the rooms upstairs, the meeting place of boys and men. But for Cellini, everything was at hand at the workshops. They were more or less private and included sleeping quarters. Warm friendships developed between the boys and young men working there, to the extent that literally anything imaginable went on. Rocke in his *Forbidden Friendships* mentions a workshop run by Francesco di Giuliano Benintendi, "full of boys" where Benintendi encouraged sodomy on the premises. For boys under 25 like Cellini Florentines considered that they were simply gaining sexual experience before marriage, around age 30.

Then Cellini became involved in a scuffle with a man, Gherardo. He hit with his open hand, but the act took place in the business section of Florence where violence was strictly forbidden. He was put in jail until he could locate another 12 bushels of flour. Finding no one who would pay it, he simply walked out of prison when everyone was away at lunchtime and went to find Gherardo, armed with a dagger. There he knifed Gherardo several times, as well as a family member also present. He fled Florence and made his way to Rome. His father went on bended knee before the court but was told that when found his son would be taken to the fields outside the walls and executed, an expeditious punishment reserved for those of insufficient wealth or connections to demand a trial.

At Rome Cellini learned of the pope's death and his replacement by Clement VII. He also learned of an obscure law that a crime committed between the death of a pope and the election of a new pope would be forgiven. He immediately found a new workshop and commissions. He took a boy of 14, Paulino, as assistant, "perfect manners, honest and the prettiest face I've seen in all my life. He's shown great love for me and my love for him is almost more than I can bear." (I told you his memoirs were clear.) And he continues: "I'm not surprised about all those stories of the Greeks and their gods. If Paulino had lived then he would have driven them all crazy." Paulino also had a sister who seems to have interested him, the first such occurrence in his writings. At the same time, he studied the works of Raphael and Sodoma. (More about Sodoma later.)

He opened his own workshop, as age 23. One of his first wealthy clients was Giacomo Bergenario da Carpi, a doctor who made his fortune treating syphilis, called the French disease because it entered Italy at the same time as Charles VIII (Part II). Da Carpi ordered some cups, the beauty of which brought in even more clients. That didn't stop Cellini from continuing his studies, especially in enamelling. Around this time a friend brought a prostitute to a supper where Cellini was invited. Cellini didn't care for her, but she was accompanied by a girl of 13. His friend retired with the whore,

Cellini with the girl and, he writes, "I had a wonderful time." He had tried to keep clean all his life, but perhaps she hadn't, as he came down with the plague.

Cared for by Giovanni Rigoli, the boy who had been accused with him of raping a younger lad, he was one of the rare survivors. To celebrate his cure, he entered a club made up of artists like himself, out for a good time. One of them was Giulio Romano, the painter of the *I Modi* sexual-intercourse drawings whom we met in the chapter on Raphael. The men thought it would be amusing to have a dinner in which they invited their mistresses. Cellini had none, but he did have a boy of wondrous beauty, 16, whom he dressed as a girl. She is recorded to have made such a splash that one of the mistress left in a huff, followed by another when one of the men put his hand in the little lady's panties and discovered the truth. The men broke up in laughter and Diego, the "girl" of wondrous beauty, was said to have passed an equally wondrous night. (The details of which, alas, are not found in Cellini's book.)

The Sack of Rome followed, most of which is in the chapter on Michelangelo, but Cellini played his part. As the undisciplined troops of Charles V descended on Rome, Cellini withdrew into the Castel Sant'Angelo with Clement VII. Modestly, this is what he says about his role in defending the pope: "All I need say is that it was thanks to me that the castle was saved." He was 27 and had lost none of his youthful verve and enthusiasm. One man present at the time who later told the story of Cellini's participation was the goldsmith Raffaello da Montelupó who, when the fighting began, was in bed with boy, the beautiful Vica d'Agobio. Raffaello immediately joined Cellini behind the canon Cellini manned, a cannon that he aimed at a Spanish officer who was in the midst of giving orders for the digging of a mine under the castle. He was blown to pieces. The pope, hearing this, ordered Cellini to his side where he absolved him from all past and present killings. Somewhere outside the Castel his brother Cecchino was also wielding arms, but as a professional. Cellini wrote that he too was now trying to decide whether to give up art in favor of arms, as he was thoroughly enjoying himself. It was during this period that a number of jewels went missing, the theft of which would be blamed on Cellini, at a later time, with dire consequences.

When Clement surrendered to Charles V, Cellini returned to Florence where he learned that the father who had always loved him more than life itself had died of the plague. During his mourning Cellini received word from Clement that his services were needed in Rome. He turned over the keys to the workshop he had founded while in Florence to a former lover, Piero Landi, son of a banker, who had brought him 10 ducats so that he could escape Florence after killing Gherardo.

We'll now get to the role and death of Alessandro de' Medici, the bastard son of Clement VII, whom Clement had named to rule Florence. We met him in the chapter on Michelangelo, but as Cellini played a part in the duke's life, we'll go on with him here and now. To seal his rule over Florence, Alessandro needed the benediction of the pope who was also his father, Clement VII. So he descended to Rome to visit Dad, accompanied by a group of boys, louts like him, who came up against even trashier men, the pope's own guard. Among Alessandro's boys was none other than Cecchino, Cellini's brother. The pope's guard arrested one of Alessandro's men—we don't know under what pretense, but Alessandro and his ruffians were known for everything, including the mass rape of nuns. The arrested boy, Bertino Aldobrandi, was a friend of Cecchino's—who, like his brother, nurtured extremely intimate friendships with his pals. Cecchino learned, falsely as it turned out, that his friend had been killed by the guard. Mad with fury, Cecchino got a description of the man he thought to be the murderer, found him, and struck him down with such force, Derek Parker tells us, that his sword was stuck in the ground and couldn't be pulled out. Another guard then shot Cecchino in the leg with an arquebus. Cellini happened to be near and ran to his brother's side. He had the boy transported to a nearby house where both brothers were met by Alessandro himself. Dying, Cecchino told Alessandro that his only regret was that he could no longer be with him to prove his loyalty and love. Cellini had him buried in the church of San Giovanni dei Fiorentini, and a beautiful memorial stone placed above his head.

Clement wanted Cellini to return to work despite his mourning for his brother, saying that Ceccino was now dead and nothing more could be done. But Italians are extremely bound to their families, and Cellini no lesser so. He found out who had shot the boy and, as he wrote, ''followed him as closely as though he were an unfaithful mistress.'' He attacked him with a dagger, a first blow that grazed the neck as the man, aware of an approaching figure, was able to move slightly out of the way. He tried to run but Cellini was on him like a lion on a fleeing antelope, downing him with another blow, to the back, and as he lay on the ground, another and still another to the neck and upper back. He then ran to Alessandro's palace near the Piazza Navona where guards caught up with him. Alessandro explained the motive for the killing and the guards left. Later, the pope simply asked him if he ''had gotten over it now'', and gave him a commission. Cellini had again murdered, and again gotten off scot-free.

We're now going to embark on a strang incident in Cellini's life. There was absolutely no doubt that Cellini liked girls, as shown through his sculptures that were not merely men with breast attached, as were Michelangelo's. And at that moment he just happened to fall in love with a certain Angelica who was kept from him by her mother who found a simple goldsmith unworthy. So Cellini found a priest who would help him get her through necromancy. Necromancy was a form of magic involving communication with the dead. As a round area was needed for the rites, he and the priest and a virgin boy retired to the Colosseum in the dead of night. A virgin boy was necessary as the spirits had no genitals and so were jealous of those who were able to use theirs for pleasure. As this was not the case of a virgin boy, they could be called to him without resentment. Using incantations and incense, the priest called up the spirits. Cellini tells us that he saw nothing, but that they boy saw the spirits and Cellini was forced to comfort him by holding him pressed to his body (that the boy was also naked was fortuitous to Cellini's urge to bring him comfort.) The spirits told Cellini, through the boy, that his request for the girl would be granted. A while later Cellini was in another row with a jeweler, a certain Capitaneis, with whom he was in competition. Words were exchanged and Cellini scooped up some mud and threw it at him. (As Caesar had splattered Marcus Bibulus, centuries before, with excrement in the senate.) Cellini *says* that unknown to him, there was a stone in the mud and the jeweler was felled. Then a few days later, while sitting with friends outside a shop, Capitaneis happened to pass with some friends. Seeing Cellini, insults and gestures were exchanged (the equivalent of giving the finger). Capitaneis and friends wandered off down the street, giggling. Cellini, despite his own friends who tried to stop him, followed Capitaneis and cold-bloodedly knifed him from behind. Capitaneis' companions had been too surprised to intervene. Cellini is said to have coolly walked away, but when news got to the pope, Cellini's arrest and execution were ordered. Alessandro nevertheless gave him a horse for his escape. He rode towards Naples when low and behold, in a tavern, he came upon Angelica. I'm certain that they passed what was, for Cellini, a wonderful night. The couple continued to Naples where they were joined by her mother, and as both daughter and mother kept trying to wrest more money from Cellini than he was willing to pay, he fled. Three days later Pope Clement was dead.

Incredibly, unbelievably, everyone then vied to protect the multi-murderer. Cardinal Francesco Cornaro convinced Cellini to take refuge in his palazzo. Then Ippolito de' Medici insisted on taking him in. When Alessandro was named to rule Florence by his father Pope Clement (at age 19), Ippolito, 17, a cousin, was named by the pope--who had raised the boy after his father's death--to second Alessandro. He was a lout like his cousin, but he knew Cellini well and now came to his aid. To keep the peace, Cellini left the cardinal's palazzo under cover of night and went to Ippolito's palace to explain to him why it would be more politically acceptable for him to remain with Cornaro. Ippolito agree. If this weren't support enough, the newly elected pope, Paul III, gave Cellini a pardon and a commission, saying, "Men like Cellini, unique to art, are above the law." But a problem arose: the pope's son, Pierluigi Farnese, "a notorious sodomite, said to have raped the bishop of Fano," Derek Parker tells us, was a friend of the man Cellini had murdered, a man who had a daughter that Farnese wanted to marry to his lover, a young peasant boy, in order to confiscate the girl's dowry (one wouldn't dare invent such a scenario even in train-station fiction). Despite what the pope felt for Cellini, Farnese had the power to order Cellini's arrest, which he did. He also hired an assassin to kill Cellini. The assassin met him in a tavern and, seduced by his charm, told Cellini of the plot to kill him. Cellini then immediately flew to Florence and the open arms of Alessandro de' Medici.

Alessandro took advice from no one, living for his own pleasure, his motto being "They made me duke, so I'll enjoy it!" By enjoying it he meant wandering the streets at night fully armed, pushing aside anyone in his way, looking for a fight he was destined to win for the simple reason that he had barred the carrying of a sword or a firearm, both of which never left him, nor did his dagger. And he had reason to fear, as the nobility of Florence wanted him replaced by legitimate blood, noble blood. He had gained power at age 19 and had by now fully tasted every perversion, so that what was left was taking the hymen of those who still had one, notably nuns, and that of those who kept guard over theirs, virtuous women. He liked his boys too, for quick, easy couplings, as heated and virile as possible. His favorite companion was his cousin Lorenzino with whom he shared his bed and more when not extinguished from a night of whoring and when he awoke with a lustful urge, Lorenzino was always conveniently spread out, naked, at his side. This is how Cellini had caught them many times, as the artist was permitted to come and go as he wished, and as Alessandro had no modesty and no need to hide his vices, Cellini was aware of every thing that went on.

Lorenzino, at times, behind his back, was called Lorenzaccio, "bad Lorenzo," for his habit of cutting off the heads of statues and other misdemeanors, clear proof that he shared much of Alessandro's brutality, at least at the beginning. Lorenzino is extremely famous in France thanks to the chef-d'oeuvre by Musset, *Lorenzaccio*:

Lorenzo: *Dormez-vous Seigneur?*

The Duke: *C'est toi, Renzo?*

Lorenzo: *Seigneur, n'en doutez pas.* And he plunges the a dagger into the duke's body.

Scoronconcolo: *Est-ce fait?*

Lorenzo: *Regarde, il m'a mordu au doigt. Je garderai jusqu'à la mort cette bague sanglante, inestimable diamant.*

No one knows why Lorenzino turned against Duke Alessandro, aided by a professional assassin, Scoronconcolo. In his play Musset writes that he wanted the duke dead so that Florence could become a Republic again. Others suggest that he was just jealous of the duke's powers and privileges. As Duke Alessandro was so unpopular, he was never without his body armor, weapons and guards. But Lorenzino told him that he had found a Florentine lady of exception beauty and, especially, ironclad virtue, who had been abandoned by her husband. Lorenzino would bring her to the duke, and from then on it was up to the duke to prove that he could triumph over virtue. Lorenzino convinced the duke to dismiss the guards for the night, to take off his armor and to slip naked into bed. From then on it was easy for Lorenzino to strike him with a dagger. Afterwards he rode off to Venice, a glove covering a finger Alessandro had nearly bitten off. There, he published his version of what had taken place in his *Apologia*, claiming to be a second Brutus. Lorenzino himself was later stabbed to death by a poisoned dagger on a bridge in Venice.

Cellini returned to Rome with still another friend, Piero, a boy of "extreme personal beauty." There Pope Paul III reassured him that he was again a free man and offered him still more commissions. At the same time he learned that he had somehow given offence to Vasari whom we've met many times thanks to his absolutely essential *Lives of the Most Excellent Painters, Sculptors and Architects.* Cellini didn't know the reason for his change of humor, especially as he had provided Vasari with boys, one of which, Manno, Vasari had badly scratched during his passion. As for Cellini: "The most handsome boy in Rome," a certain Ascanio, replaced Piero in his affections. Ascanio didn't last long because, as Cellini put it, the boy succumbed to "a girl who put her hand down his trousers and he seemingly enjoyed it."

The breakup with Ascanio didn't last long either, however, and it was lucky for Cellini as Cellini was arrested due to his enemy Farnese who dug up the accusation that Cellini had stolen jewels from Clement during the Sack of Rome. He got his father Paul III to have Cellini thrown in jail. It was Ascanio who visited him daily, bringing news and fresh food. And then disaster. Leaving Castel Sant'Angelo Ascanio was attacked by enemies of Cellini, perhaps sent by Farnese, and only escaped by wounding several with his dagger. He was forced to flee to his native Tagliacozzo where Ascanio, whom Cellini described as so handsome that no one could resist him, sent a tearful letter of explanation to his lover.

From then on the world went black for Cellini. In trying to escape from Castel Sant'Angelo by a knotted sheet, he fell and very badly broke his leg. While his leg was being cared for, he tried to escape again, this time hiding himself in a mattress, carried out of the city by a friend, a Greek, who just happened to have been young and handsome, wrote Cellini. The plan was foiled and Cellini sent to the notorious prison the Tor di Nona where for months he lived in squalor, the earth floor the habitat of insects and rats, his mattress soaked with the ambient dampness, the food not only disgusting but, Cellini feared, poisoned by Farnese. With time he became delusional, visited by angels, naked beautiful boys who pleaded with him to not commit suicide, boys he sketched on the prison walls with a piece of charcoal he found on the floor. Why Paul III kept him in such squalor is unknown. The pope was known to drink far to heavily and his problems with Henry VIII ended with the king being excommunicated and the country placed under interdict, meaning no more masses, burials, confessions and marriages. The world stopped turning under interdict, except for Henry who simply invented a religion of his own making, and the people of England went along. At any rate, the least that one could say about Cellini was that in the pope's eyes he was very small potatoes.

Then a miracle. Cellini had met Cardinal Ippolito d'Este (whose uncle had married Lucrezia Borgia and, you may remember from Part II, rode around town at night with his sword in one hand, his erect cock in the other) in Rome. A lover of boys and age 28 at the time, he had been fascinated by the artist. Now Ippolito was dining with the pope and when Paul was seriously drunk Ippolito asked him why he was keeping Cellini a prisoner. Paul said he didn't give a hoot for Cellini and if Ippolito wanted to, he could take Cellini home with him that very night. Which is exactly what Ippolito did. He took him home at 4 a.m. after freeing him from prison. Both the cardinal and Cellini thought that other horizons would be better for his health, so he packed up Ascanio, the most handsome boy in Rome, and a new lad, age 14, Pietro Pagolo, and the threesome headed for Fontainebleau and a lad who had already lost his virginity to his sister at age 10, a lad 6 foot ½ tall and so big some girls couldn't accommodate him although most tried, and, it was said, virgins literally lined up around his bed awaiting their chance to be deflowered—his specialty. The bed even accompanied him while he was out hunting, using it between kills, to the utter amazement of Henry VIII who had accompanied the king during his visit to France (Henry went far in such things, very far even, but not *that* far). The lad was François I. François took whomever he wanted from the nobility, whether the ladies liked it or not, and apparently not all did as one woman had her husband infect himself with syphilis before infecting her so that she could infect the king. Another woman had her face slashed, which didn't dissuade François as it wasn't her face that interested him. But he also brought the Renaissance to France (he had cradled the head of the dying da Vinci) and Cellini was a great catch.

A great deal of Cellini's time was wasted in Fontainebleau, some due to the artist's dallying, a lot due to François who was at war with Henry VIII and Charles V and couldn't find time for Benvenuto, time lost in disputes with other court painters and sculptors, and time lost in quarrels with François' long-term mistress, Madame d'Étampes, who thought everything was her divine right as she had held the king's interest in her cunt for a decade. (As Diane de Poitiers had captivated Henry II, and Catherine de' Medici, his wife, had drilled a hole in the wall to spy of them, to see just how she did it—Part II.) And time was lost by François who just couldn't hold still and would wander off, for no apparent reason, going from chateau to chateau, followed by an enormous train of 12,000 servants and nobles. But Cellini did complete some masterpieces, his saltcellar (which must be seen close up to really appreciate) and *The Nymph of Fontainebleau.*

No matter how beautiful were Ascanio and Pagolo, a man is programmed by nature to want more and Cellini found it in a girl, Caterina, a girl who served as model, a girl he seems to have been deeply, sexually, attached to. He did what he could to keep her out of the hands of others, fearing she might become pregnant. Alas, coming home early from a dinner he found her in flagrant delicto with a boy. In her defense, Caterina accused him of sodomy, an offense that was more or less troublesome in Italy, but one that brought death in France. He was judged and got off, but we known nothing of the hows and whys because the court records have been lost. Caterina was chased from the house, but it suddenly became clear why he didn't want her with another boy. Because Cellini used her as he did his boys, she couldn't become pregnant. And if she ever did, she could sue him because he obviously couldn't have risked having his head cut off by telling the court that he had used her anally.

Now we have to touch on an unfortunate side of his life, unfortunate for me because I've come to love this man. He was incredibly vindictive. One known story about him took place in a tavern where he and a lad had stopped for the night. The tavern keeper asked to be paid in advance, an unusual practice as one paid when one left. To the displeasure of the boy sharing his bed, Cellini spent the night ranting about the tavern keeper. After leaving the next day he circled back, slipped upstairs to his old room, and cut the bedding to pieces. For good measure, he scarred the woodwork and chest of drawers with his dagger. Of course, this was of little consequence compared to his murderous nature, but murder can most often be explained by unfortunate incidents in one's life, especially one's childhood. Alas, we do not know enough about Cellini's to know what motivated his sudden and very deadly furies. We know his father genuinely adored him, and one feels that that should have been sufficient. Also, the times he lived in were in themselves incredibly violent where one word too much, one angry look, could end in a death or deaths. That said, when we see the equally incredible violence in today's video games, played by millions, one realizes that the beast is there, just under the surface of us all. That sermon aside, what he did next is, to me at least, inexplicable.

Obsessed by Caterina, we went to her boyfriend's house where he found the boy and Caterina together. He pulled out his dagger and placed it against the boy's throat and told him that if he and Caterina didn't marry immediately, he'd slit the boy's throat. The lad, terrified, agreed. This bit of revenge accomplished, he left. The marriage took place and Cellini, finding that he really did still desire her, invited Caterina to return to model for him. She did and they were soon back in bed together. At first his friends thought that Cellini was just out to avenge himself by cuckolding the boy; they thought Caterina had returned because she needed the money and the ample meals Cellini provided for his assistants. But it was more than that. He began beating her and even admitted in his book, ''I would pull her by her hair, all across the room, kick her and give her blows until I was tired out. Her clothes were ripped and she would be bloody and her legs swollen.'' Then they'd make love. Then she'd model for him. Then he'd attack her again. I suppose any psychiatrist could explain this behavior, but I can't. As for boys, he wasn't afraid of them, yet he never ever threatened them in this way. He used women and showed love and affection for the boys he lived with, treating them as companions, happy in their company when having sex and when not having sex.

Things grew worse with Madame d'Étampes. The king ordered some candle bearers, statues as tall as the king, over six feet. After months, he produced one, a male figure, with a bit of tissue covering its genitals. When Madame d'Étampes suggested to the king that the tissue was there to hid some imperfection, Cellini had Ascanio take it away. Madame d'Étampes stared at the incredible detail of the pubic bush, balls, penis and ample foreskin, and Cellini asked, ''Do you find it all as it should be?'' Madame d'Étampes left the room in a huff and as soon as she was gone the king ''exploded with laughter,'' says Cellini.

At this time he met another girl, Scorzone, whom he claimed was a virgin and with whom he had a baby girl. He mentions her just once in his autobiography and nothing more. Later, in France, he would have a baby boy who was taken from the mother and given to a wet-nurse, the wife of one of his assistants. We never learn the name of the woman who bore his child, but he did care for the boy until he was accidently smothered by his nurse.

As Madame d'Étampes succeeded in poisoning the king's mind against Cellini because of his cold indifference to her and his unwillingness to kowtow, relations worsened. Finally Cellini decided to return to Florence. He left Ascanio and Pagolo in charge of his workshop. Here the boys who had served him so well disappeared from history, but my little finger tells me they certainly married and founded a family, for Florentines were very rarely exclusively male oriented like Michelangelo and da Vinci. I hope they had a fulfilling end of life, I sincerely, tearfully do.

He returned to Florence where Cosimo had now ruled for eight years and was living in the Palazzo della Signoria, by far the most beautiful palazzo in Florence. Disturbed by the smell of meat sold on the Ponte Vecchio, he had the butchers replaced by jewelers, as it is today. Cosimo promised that if Cellini produced a great work of art, he would not be disappointed in his reward. Sadly, Cosimo I did not follow in the footsteps of his ancestor, the first Cosimo discussed in Part II. He was a know-it-all who paid laborers' wages, when he paid something at all. On the other hand, some artists demanded ridiculous sums for their works, and only after payment was made did the buyer find he had been badly taken advantage of. So it was often a case of once bitten twice shy. In this Cellini might not have always been as honest as Caesar's wife, but at any rate he completely lacked Michelangelo's gold touch in the commerce of his oeuvre, which earned Michelangelo great wealth. Speaking of Michelangelo, Cosimo would certainly have chosen him over Cellini, who was not noted as yet for his sculptures, but the great Buonarroti was busy in the Vatican.

Cellini suggested doing the statue of Perseus, Cosimo agreed, a place for it was rapidly found, in front of Cosimo's home, the Palazzo della Signoria, facing Michelangelo's *David*. A new boy, handsome, naturally, was found too, a very young lad, Cencio, son of a prostitute who would eventually accuse him of sodomizing her boy in an attempt to extract money, but for the moment that lay in the future. He took on Bernardino Manelli, the exquisite head and body of whom would be the model for the future *Perseus*, and other young assistants whose horizons he enlarged by taking them to the Old Market, the Chaisso de' Buoi, the Tavern Buca and the baths, all pleasure zones where the lads could enjoy both sexes, singly or in bacchanals. Bernardino turned out to be intelligent, loyal and hard working, and was Cellini's first assistant from then on.

Perseus would take Cellini nine years, much of it lost in disputes with Cosimo, lost while doing some minor commissions, here and there, lost due to other artists who tried to turn the duke against him, and lost because of his being obliged to flee Florence when Cencio's mom said she'd bring the law on his head if he didn't find the means to dissuade her. He went off to Venice with Bernardino where, incredibly, he met up with Lorenzino, Alessandro's assassin, whose own destiny would soon come to an instant halt at the end of a dagger. But for the moment all three shared the limitless vices of the Republic of the Doges. Cellini was his own worse enemy, in the sense that at times he just didn't want to work, and at other times he was busy elsewhere doing things like impregnating girls whose names he doesn't even mention in his book, even though two of them presented him with two new sons. Back in Florence he did, nonetheless, cast two very important busts, one of a banker, Altoviti, and another of, naturally, Cosimo himself. Artists seem to prefer Altoviti's sculpture, but my favorite is clearly that of

Cosimo. You can decide for yourself thanks to the Net where you'll find all of Cellini's other works, especially François' saltcellar in color that brings out the fabulous use of enamel.

If you've read my *HOMOSEXUALITY, The True Lives of the Fabulous Men who Preferred Men—Volume One—The Ancient Greeks*, as well as my *TROY*, then you know that I'm mad about Greek mythology. But frankly, the story of Perseus isn't all that passionate: Acrisius, King of Argos, wanted a son and consulted the Delphic Oracle who told him that his *daughter* would have a boy, but that the boy would grow up and kill Acrisius. So Acrisius locked away his daughter who was nonetheless impregnated by Zeus who took the form of a golden shower (?). The son she bore was Perseus. Acrisius refused to kill them both so instead locked them in a chest that he flung into the sea. The chest was netted by fishermen loyal to King Polydectes who reared Perseus. Polydected wanted to marry Perseus' mother but Perseus refused him her hand, telling the king he would give him whatever else he wanted. The king said he would settle for the Gorgon Medusa, a monster having a terrible face and hair of serpents, a face so horrible that the person looking on it froze with fright. The gods favored Perseus and gave him a sack in which to put the head, winged feet to get to it, a sickle to cut it off, and the helmet of invisibility belonging to Hades. Perseus collected the head and returned (after profuse adventures) to Polydectes who said he had sent the boy away to be killed by the Medusa, and had never planned to give up his mother. Perseus opened the sack, looked the other way, and froze Polydectes to stone. He then returned to Argos where, during Olympic-style games, he threw a discus that rebounded and killed Acrisius. (Whew!)

That's what Cellini was to sculpt ... and this is how he went about it: Cellini built a clay core of the approximate size and shape of the intended statue. The clay core was then coated with wax, and vents were added to facilitate the flow of molten metal and allow gases to escape so that the casting would be uniform. Next the wax was completely covered in an outer layer of clay. The whole was heated so that the wax melted and flowed away through the vents. At the same time the outer clay was hardened. This done, molten bronze was poured into the mold until the space between the clay core and the outer clay covering was filled up, entirely replacing where the wax had been. When the bronze had cooled, the outer clay mould was chipped away and the bronze was ready for the finishing process. The problem was that the bronze didn't always get into every nook and cranny. In *Perseus'* case one of the feet had to be recast as the bronze hadn't completely descended into it.

An added detail: The cast had been heated for 48 hours, time for the wax to melt away and for the clay mould to bake. Then the whole thing, incredibly heavy, was lowered into a huge hole and covered with packed earth so that the clay mould wouldn't break while the bronze was being poured. The whole was left to cool for two days. The result even surprised Cellini and was a shock to Cosimo who had predicted that it would never turn out. In fact, his meddling was such that several times Cellini said he would leave Florence and return to François, knowing that this was out of the question because although he had problems with Cosimo and other artists who badmouthed him through jealousy, there was still Madame d'Étampes who would pester him to death.

Under the statue Cellini created a pedestal adorned by smaller statues, one of his lover Cencio, a young scamp totally naked and eminently desirable, who had shared his bed since age 12. The Medusa herself was his model Dorotea who also shared his bed and who gave him a son he legitimized. All told, Cellini was living and creating, creating and living, in the most beautiful city in the world, under skies warmed by the unstinting generosity of Helios, his *Perseus* complete, his immortality guaranteed.

He went off on vacation for a few weeks with a new boy, Cesare. On his return he opened the head of a fellow goldsmith, Lorenzo Papi, for reasons unknown, and was sent to the terrible prison of Stinche from whence Cosimo had him released. And then an apprentice, Ferrando di Giovanni da Montepulciao, accused him of "sexual intercourse on many occasions," a boy he seemed to have loved, one he had put in his will before some unknown disagreement separated them. "I take back everything I've done for him," Cellini wrote, "He'll receive nothing. His name will vanish from my will." Here Cellini was forced to plead guilty because Ferrando produced witnesses who had actually seen them at it. Cellini was sentenced to four years in jail but again Cosimo intervened. He received a year of house arrest instead. He then begot another child, a boy, from an unnamed servant, and then still more children by a model, Piera de' Salvatore Parigi, whom he married.

He went to work on his book which, next to *Perseus*, was his greatest triumph. He weakened. He died, accompanied to his resting place by hoards of admirers—I can't say *last* resting place because, for this man who had never stopped moving, it was, in reality, his first. Years ago, when I entered the Peace Corps, I received a huge box of books, as do all volunteers. One was *The Autobiography of Benvenuto Cellini*. I read it with great pleasure, totally unaware of the volcano who had produced it, only vaguely aware of my own sexuality, never dreaming that I would eventually, like countless other boys, fall in love with this incredible creature, proof that God does work in entirely mysterious ways.

PART VIII

CARAVAGGIO

Historians writing about Caravaggio go off on tangents—interesting and instructive tangents—such as the life of this or that pope existent at the time, the supposed influence of this or that cardinal or priest on the artist, none of whom had, in reality, the tiniest hold on Caravaggio, because if they had had such a role, how could one explain the painter's violence and the murders attributed to him? The truth of Caravaggio is that once all we know about him is boiled down, it is reduced like a gallon of alcohol and a basketful of roses passing through a distiller, and what we're left with is the scent emitting from a few residual drops. As his story struck a cord in me, I read several biographies, all long, some very long, absent of nearly all detail concerning his passage on earth. Naturally, there was plenty of discussion centered on his paintings, but I'm not gifted in this kind of analysis and, anyway, I'd rather just admire them in a museum ambiance. What I'm getting at is that this chapter, like the book itself, will be a concentration of every ''living'' detail I can find about the man, ''living'' in the sense of alive, vibrant, of intense human interest. And although we may know little, what we do know is simply incredible.

He lost nearly every male member of his family to the plague while still very young, the plague that had killed over half of the population of Italy a generation earlier, around the 1350s, but reappeared from time to time to claim the survivors. This might have instilled a sentiment of abandonment, a child's first and greatest fear, a scar on the mind that pushes one incessantly from place to place, person to person, never at ease, never satisfied, always angry, violent, physically and sexually aggressive. Perhaps only a man of such unhinged and brutal appetites could create the works of this totally unique individual, stark, aggressive and sexually explosive works of art. This may partially explain the brutality of his nature, as well as the fact that the times in which he lived were in themselves ultraviolent, where even if a man looked at another for a nanosecond too long he might be challenged and put to death by sword. Some say too that a catalyst for his brutal character stemmed simply from the chemicals used in his painting, lead white and vermillion, both of which are highly toxic.

Caravaggio was a man of great strength and a first-class swordsman. That he was also an artist whose delicate strokes created works of genius must not mask the fact of his indomitable virility, capable of downing a man with a blow--temporarily if done with the fist, life-threatening at the end of his sword. The proof of this was his slaying of the handsome Ranuccio Tomassoni in a sword duel. Caravaggio ran with a pack of toughs, armed to the hilt in a city where arms were forbidden. He and his goons drank and whored, pushed fellow revelers aside as they made their way through the allies from tavern to tavern. They were constantly picked up by the Roman police, held the night and then freed as they had powerful friends, friends like Cardinal del Monte who was smitten by boys and who appreciated homoerotic art, bringing much of it into the Vatican (one of the reasons why the Vatican is, today, a must-see museum). He allowed Caravaggio to bed Cecco, a boy of only ten when he appeared as a prepubescent *St. John the Baptist*, a beautiful, brooding lad when painted a handful of years later in another *St. John.* He and his ruffians broke windows, sang bawdy songs, hurled animal bladders filled with blood or ink at buildings, smeared excrement on door handles and, naturally, drew erect, usually discharging phalluses on walls. An unknown source had this to say at the time: ''After a fortnight's work he swaggers about for a month or two with a sword and like-minded friends at this side--Prospero Orsi, Constantino Spata, Mario Minniti and Onorio Longhi--ever ready to engage in a fight or an argument, so that it is awkward to get along with him.'' Another of his acquaintances, Agostino Tassi, was accused by a father of ''repeatedly deflowering'' his daughter! (Perhaps, like Aphrodite, her virginity continually returned by bathing off the shores of Cyprian Paphos.)

He whored, but his preference was men, a choice far from unknown in the Florence of his epoch where men chose freedom over marital bondage, where one could take one's pleasure when and where one desired, with a boy or a man, free of nagging and the expense of a meal. This is what Andrew Graham-Dixon says in his wonderful *Caravaggio*: ''Caravaggio was capable of being aroused by the physical presence of other men. He could not have painted such figures in the way that he did if that were not so. Caravaggio's painting suggests an ambiguous sexual personality. On the evidence of his paintings he was neither heterosexual nor homosexual, terms that are in any case anachronistic when applied to his world. He was omnisexual.'' This makes Graham-Dixon's book the most even-handed approach to the subject I've read, as most authors go out of their way to presume a man innocent of homoerotic yearnings and—even more—of committing homosexual acts unless provided with the proof of their guilt by someone having spent the night under the perpetrator's bed.

Boys at that time loved to dress to kill. Churches abounded in Renaissance Italy, and especially in Florence and Milan, perfect stages for a young sire to show off his splendid forms, silk-adorned chest, form-fitting trousers, elegance out to swoon the fair sex, a dagger at the belt and a sword ever handy, a youth's tools. For the daily, reliable and rapid purging of one's lust, there were bordellos, taverns with frisky and economically cheap servers, as well as back alleys where, indeed, all cats were grey in the absence of light, and a lad had but to pull the strings attached to the cloth that covered his private parts to take his pleasure with whomever engorged his manhood, or when he simply wished to relieve himself against a wall.

Michelangelo Merisi da Caravaggio was born around 1571. Famous while he lived, he was immediately forgotten after his death, to be rediscovered in the twentieth century. He was blessed with two beautiful names, *Michelangelo* which evoked the famous Florentine genius, although Caravaggio's first name had been chosen after the feast day on which he had been born, Archangel Michael, and *Caravaggio*, the site of his birth. His father was a mason, but one with important connections, thanks to the nobility for whom he worked. One person especially stands out, Constanza Colonna, from the Colonna family of military glory, who took an interest in the son of her servant. We'll meet her later when she comes to the rescue of Caravaggio, but for the moment she weds, at age 12, Francesco Sforza, 17, a marriage that starts off so poorly that she threatens to kill herself if her father doesn't free her: "If you don't get me out of his house I'll kill myself and my lost soul be damned!" As the Colonna carried weight, the pope allowed her to enter a nunnery where she gave birth to a son (I haven't found the key to this enigma, unless it was, quite simply, a miracle). Five other sons followed, perhaps signifying that she had somehow found her husband less boorish than at first. Alas, two of her boys would turn out to be as uncontrollable as Caravaggio.

A two-hour ride from the stiflingly dead town of Caravaggio brought one to the big city, Milan, under Spanish rule at the time, the bustling center of commerce and manufacturing, 100,000 souls--as many as London and Paris--and the epicenter of the silk industry as well as the finest workmanship in swords and daggers in the world, a world inhabited by the young Caravaggio until he went to Florence at the age of 21. Florence was the capital of art, and da Vinci and Michelangelo were its kings. What a change Caravaggio would bring to all this. Already Michelangelo was known for his nudes, the genitals of which would be later painted over. But how different were his nudes from Caravaggio's. Michelangelo's muscular lads looked as fresh and scrubbed as if they'd just stepped out of an hour-long shower. Caravaggio's boys were so realistic that one could nearly whiff the pheromones from the lads' beautiful but slightly rank bodies, and in his *Jupiter, Neptune and Pluto* we have a full under view of Neptune's pubic push, scrotum and penis with its full prepuce. I insist on this point: the boys in his pictures are totally alive, and even when just sitting, surrounded by fruit or flowers, their shirts open over their naked chests, one has the impression that they've just left a bed after making sweet love, and that the unwashed sperm still coats their bellies. In the book *Who's Who in Gay and Lesbian History*--a marvelous book that I use only to verify the facts I've gleaned from other sources with those in the very short synopses found in *Who's Who*—the writer says that Caravaggio's *Amore vincitore* makes him think of a "completely naked pin-up teenager," which underlines the sexiness of his paintings, even though, in the case of the *Amore vincitore,* it's not at all the naked pin-up of a teenager I'd have in *my* bedroom. As far as realism goes, nothing is more ghastly than the blood spurting from the jugular vein of a tyrant, sectioned by a sword in his *Judith and Holofernes*. The realism in his paintings was such that he even showed the dirt under the toenails! But all this is the future. For the moment he's 13 and apprenticed to Simone Peterzano, a painter of mediocre repute who taught the boy little except for a smidgen of drawing and the art of grounding colors. Caravaggio's thought to have been rowdy even at that age, controlled with difficulty. He ran around with gangs as he did later in life, and he certainly had his first experiences with boys and whores. And as Milan was noted for its violence he may have done more, he may have killed someone as is suggested in several texts, but at any rate he left the city never to return, headed south to his destiny in Rome.

He was described as being handsome in a wild way, his curly, unruly hair, his eyes were large and wide like a Spaniards, his clothes said to have been of the best quality and cut, but worn until they were nearly rags. The city he entered, Rome, had once been like Caravaggio in a new array of the best clothes, it had been the center of the ancient world and had reigned supreme for half a millennium, but now it was decrepit, the buildings crumpling among fields of mud, rats and stench, with only a few favored islets inhabited by the rich and powerful. It was there Caravaggio found lodging, in the Palazzo Madama, the palace of Cardinal Francesco Maria del Monte, a man known for his paternal interest in boys in general, and homosexual artists in particular, who introduced homoerotic art into the Vatican, and was himself homosexual. The palace housed as many as fifty boys, artists like Caravaggio, actors who took part in plays dressed as women when the role demanded it, rent-boy when out of work, and castrati. He came with his luggage: a tormented mind, a character as unruly as his hair, violent fists and a sword and dagger at his side, despite their interdiction in the holy city famed for its bordellos, its clergy who feasted on the animal pursuits of the world in the form of the finest food and drink, and because they lived in palaces they needed architects, sculptures, playwrights to fill their theaters, painters like Caravaggio, and warm bodies to span their nights. One Englishman described Italians as being addicted to "the art of Epicureanism, the art of whoring, of poisoning and of sodomy." Caravaggio spent much time with his friends roaming the vicinity of the Piazza Navona and, if they wanted women, the Piazza del Popolo where women and boys plied their trade in ill-lit alleys or behind the parted curtains from their lodgings where they appeared naked, enticing men who often found that what they were buying was far more sordid than what they could get for free among their own sex. One of his early biographers, Giovanni Bellori, describes Caravaggio as being dark, dark in his looks, in his temperament and in his art, an extremely apt insight.

Another description of Caravaggio's place in Rome and Roman violence comes from Tommaso Garzoni, relayed to us by Graham-Dixon: "Every day, every hour, every moment, they talk of nothing but killing, cutting off legs, breaking arms, smashing somebody's spine ... For study, they have nothing other than the thought of killing this or that person; for purpose, nothing more than to avenge the wrongs that they have taken to heart; for favor, noting more than serving their friends by butchering enemies..." With Caravaggio we will continually go from summit to summit, one in blazing light—that of his art, the other in princely dark—his intimate nature.

He soon came to know his fellow artists against whom he fought for commissions, all of whom lived in the same vicinity, ate in the same restaurants, drank in the same taverns, and bought their supplies from the same street vendor, Antinoro Bertucci. Caravaggio started out, claims one source, by painting the heads of famous early Greeks and Romans, very popular among those climbing the ladder in society, exchanging their mercantile or militaristic origins for those of the educated nobility. Such collections had begun with Federico da Montefeltro whom we met in Part II. From there Caravaggio went on to still life's, another field just opening up, one he would combine, later on, in his paintings of young shirtless boys, like the *Boy with a Basket,* mentioned in the Introduction, holding or surrounded by flowers and fruit.

He had boys for his bed, especially Cicco whom he had known as a child and who had grown into an exquisite young man. Sodomy was punished by death, but as it was practiced as often in Rome as in Florence, rare were the persons tried for the crime, rare, at any rate, among the nobility and, even more, among the clergy. But an artist kept his lusts a secret as his commissions could suffer with this kind of taint to his reputation. Of course, none of this stopped Caravaggio who at all times, it seemed, was out for a fight. He attacked a young man, a notary, from behind as he walked along the Piazza Navona, in plain daylight, because the boy had somehow insulted him, perhaps over one of Caravaggio's girls. Profusely bleeding, the boy got to the police to tell his story, before rushing off—supposedly unaided—to the hospital. The painter wound up paying a large indemnity. Then came another episode in a restaurant where Caravaggio had ordered some artichokes, half cooked in oil, half in butter. When he asked the server which was which, the lad answered that the man had only to smell them to find out. Caravaggio took this as arrogant disrespect and hit him with the plate used to serve the artichokes, severely cutting him. He then reached for his sword but the boy had the presence of mind to flee. Here too he had to pay up. Stopped by a policeman for carrying a sword, he had, exceptionally, a permit to do so on him (permits given to high officials and their bodyguards). The policeman bid him

"Goodnight," but as he walked away Caravaggio, perhaps unhappy that an artist like himself, who knew so many great men, had been detained by a redneck officer, called him, to his back, a cocksucker, and invited the gentleman to shove his "Goodnight" up his bloody ass. He was thrown in jail but was released the next day, as he knew he would be.

After this we discover another chapter in his dark existence. Ranuccio Tomassoni had a stable of women he put on the streets. Known for his extreme good looks and for being well-endowed, his women were extremely jealous of on whom he bestowed his favors, to the point of attacking one another with daggers, hoping to scar a pretty face, or splash it with acid. The Roman police were called in numerous times to bring calm to the domestic situation. Ranuccio was always armed despite its unlawfulness, but invariably defended himself by stating that in his business being armed was necessary due to the girls' rowdy clients. At the same time, it appears that Caravaggio too had his girls who disputed their place of the streets with those of Ranuccio, the basis of an explosive situation that would lead to Caravaggio's attempt to knife the boy, perhaps aiming at his genitals but striking instead the femoral artery, a place certain to cause nearly instant death. Both Caravaggio and Ranuccio had been accompanied by three men each, Onorio Longhi was there on Caravaggio's side and a captain of the guards was with Ranuccio. He too was run through but whether he died or not is uncertain. Caravaggio was put out of action with an unfatal blow to the head. The surviving six men stated that the incident had been over an unpaid wager on a tennis match, although most probably it was a duel over prostitution, but as dueling in Rome carried the death sentence.... Caravaggio fled before his trial and was therefore sentenced to death, duel or no duel. A bounty was put on his head, a head that could literally be presented, severed from the body, in order to claim it.

Now on the run, Caravaggio left Rome with all that was precious to him, his clothes and painting materials, his money and Cecco. He went to the Palazzo Colonna where he begged Constanza Colonna, whom we met at the beginning of our story, for help, help immediately offered as he and Cecco were packed off to the Colonna estate in the Alban Hills. There he painted *David with the Head of Goliath*, David being Cecco and the head, severed from the body, Caravaggio himself, its mouth open in a silent scream. The painting was sent as a gift to Scipione Borghese, who just happened to be head of papal justice, the man who could free Caravaggio from the death penalty. Borghese was powerful, but Caravaggio's enemies more so. He was to remain in exile.

He went to Naples, an immense city of 300,000, a city as decrepit then as it is today, home to criminals, crime and rackets, to the poor and scarcely educated, among whom labored 10,000 slaves. Yet the city thrived thanks to its sleepless citizens, scholars in trade, professors of import and export. As with Milan, Naples too was under Spanish rule, and as in ancient Rome, the nobility—meaning the Spanish and the wealthy—circulated through the streets in covered litters.

He resided with the Colonna but as his reputation had preceded him, he did not need their help in securing what became a flood of commands. As in the Rome of that period, what could the rich do with their wealth, once their stomachs and loins were assuaged, other than tend to their palaces and gardens and interiors? But then word filtered through to Naples, from Rome, that Caravaggio had hired assassins to do away with his enemies, and whatever the truth of the matter, the uproar forced him to flee again, this time to Malta where thanks to the paintings he did of several Knights of Malta he gained near godlike admiration and was even knighted. But Malta was not Rome or Naples. Ruled by strict conservatives, there was no shouting in the streets and bawdy singing, no smearing of excrement on door handles, no sword and dagger play, no sexual indiscretions beyond his own bedroom. But there were nonetheless young men whose testosterone kept from kowtowing to Caravaggio in the manner he felt was his due, Caravaggio the famous artist and Knight. Violence resurfaced in this eternally tormented soul. He was involved in another fight, imprisoned and then escaped to the island of Sicily, all of which defies the imagination as the escape took place from an inescapable prison, on an inescapable island surrounded by rough seas, and unless he made a written confession that will one day come to light, we will never know anything, or very little, of all of these incredible events.

On Sicily he came upon his old bar-hoping, whore-frequenting, street-brawling pal and lover, Mario Minniti, who had calmed himself enough to establish his own well-considered workshop, earning the patronage of the island's Who's Who. In résumé, Minniti had become a gentleman. Caravaggio was again immediately besieged by commissions from the wealthy who wished to distinguish themselves by possessing one of his oeuvres. But due to the sudden presence of ships from Malta, that he felt were there to capture him, he decamped to Messina. There his assiduous presence at dockside where boys plunged and swam naked—one of them his model for still another nude *St. John the Baptist*—created an uproar, especially as the boy model had purportedly bestowed his favors on the painter, an uproar also due to the knowledge of how unacceptably easy it is for an experienced man to sweet-talk an innocent and inexperienced lad into sharing his bed. He escaped to Palermo and then back to Naples.

Good news awaited him there. The faithful Constanza Colonna had brokered a deal with Malta to drop charges against Caravaggio, probably in exchange for several paintings, and a papal pardon was in the works. Perhaps with a sigh of relief he went to the Osteria del Cerriglio, a tavern in a back alley of Naples frequented by both the dregs of society and the upper-class slumming for sex, a place known for its orgies, possessing a secret door for men who preferred boys, a door Caravaggio took as he certainly took the lad or lads within. On his way out of the tavern he was waylaid by four men who slashed his face, the punishment reserved for whores. They were thought to have been Maltese sent to punish, if not kill, the painter. Later, some put blame on the family and friends of Ranuccio Tomassoni. He recovered enough to sail to Rome where he was assured a pardon for the Ranuccio slaying. On the way he stopped at Porto Ercola (known well by me and my sailboat) where this man, so clearly cut out for a violent death by sword or dagger, came down with a fever, as Virgil had off the coast of Brindisi. The light went out for them both, an eternal loss to the world. Of the lesser players, Caravaggio's sidekick in fighting and whoring, Onorio Longhi, died of syphilis. Cecco took the name Cecco del Michelangelo and vanished from history, having lived a life of infinite rebounds, sharing the air and more with this fabulous, enigmatic artist. Constanza Colonna was faithful to the end, exactly what end I'm unaware of. But she's earned a place in my heart until my own end which I hope-- like that requested by Caesar the night before his assassination, while dining with Brutus--will be rapid and unexpected.

But my life is of importance only to me. The life of the choleric genius enriched humanity, affixing his seal until the end of time. He was a man who certainly abused life, but one that allowed life, in its turn, to use him— for me the paramount accolade.

His end was the befitting dream of any man, for he was accompanied by his beloved Cecco, as Achilles had accompanied Patroclus, as Alexander had accompanied his cherished Hephaestion, and as Salaì and Melzi had accompanied da Vinci.

POSTSCRIPT

So now we leave the Renaissance and Italy--Italy the Eternal--and its greatest wonders, its artists, sculptors, painters, writers, and their assistants and apprentices and models, Italy's warriors, the likes of Cesare and Cellini's little brother Ceccino, Italy's athletes, none mentioned, alas, during the Renaissance, but certainly visible today, Italy's politicians, beginning with Lorenzo *Il Magnifico*, Italy's humanists, the greatest of whom was Lorenzo's grandfather, Cosimo, and all that is and was glorious to this glorious land: in a word, its boys.

SOURCES FOR THE ITALIAN RENAISSANCE

Ady Cecilia, *A History of Milan under the Sforza,* 1907
Aldrich Robert and Garry Wotherspoon, *Who's Who in Gay and Lesbian*

History, 2001

Bicheno Hugh, *Vendetta, High Art and Low Cunning at the Birth of the Renaissance*, 2007

Bramly Serge, *Leonardo*, 1988. I hesitated to order the book due to its date of publication, but that would have been a great mistake as it's not only beautifully written, it's marvelously complete. Bramly, no prude, covers in depth da Vinci's homosexuality. An absolute must.

Cawthorne, Nigel, *Sex Lives of the Popes*, 1996

Chamberlin, E.R. *The Fall of the House of Borgia*, 1974

Cloulas Ivan, *The Borgia*, 1989

Forellino Antonio, *Michelangelo*, 2005. The most beautiful reproductions I've ever seen in a book, but nearly nothing about Michelangelo's homosexuality.

Gayford Martin, *Michelangelo*, 2013. A beautiful book, wonderfully written. Michelangelo's homosexuality so evenhandedly covered that I had to look up Gayford to see if he was gay—with a wife and children he apparently isn't. A must, must read.

Johnson, Marion, *The Borgias*, 1981

Graham-Dixon Andrew, *Caravaggio*, 2010. The book is fabulous. A genuine I-couldn't-put-it-down.

Grazia Sebastian de, *Machiavelli in Hell*, 1989

Guicciardini, *Storie fiorentine (History of Florence)*, 1509. An absolute must-read.

Hibbert Christopher, *The Borgias and Their Enemies*, 2009. I buy and love everything he writes.

Hibbert Christopher, *The Rise and Fall of the House of Medici*, 1974

Hibbert Christopher, *Florence, the Biography of a City*, 1993

Landucci Luca, *A Florentine Diary*, around 1500, an apothecary who wrote about Florence and is today a vital source concerning his times.

Lev Elizabeth, *The Tigress of Forli*, 2011. Wonderfully written. I love Elizabeth Lev for having giving us this marvelous work about this incredible woman.

Lubkin Gregory, *A Renaissance Court*, 1994

Manchester William, *A World Lit Only By Fire*, 1993

Martines Lauro, *April Blood-Florence and the Plot against the Medici*, 2003. A magnificent book, I've reread it three times.

Meyer G.J. *The Borgias, The Hidden History*, 2013

Noel Gerard, *The Renaissance Popes*, 2006

Parker Derek, *Cellini*, 2003, the book is beautifully written and full of reproductions. The very, very best on this fabulous artist.

Rocke Michael, *Forbidden Friendships*, 1996, both indispensible and wonderful. Rocke has become *incontournable*.

Sabatini Rafael, *The Life of Cesare Borgia*, 1920

Saslow James, *Ganymede in the Renaissance*, 1986

Simonetta Marcello, *The Montefeltro Conspiracy*, 2008. Wonderful, wonderful, wonderful.

Strathern Paul, *The Medici, Godfathers of the Renaissance*, 2003, An absolute must-read.

Unger Miles, *Machiavelli*, 2008

Unger Miles, *Magnifico, The Brilliant Life and Violent Times Of Lorenzo de' Medici*, 2011. Wonderful. The best.

Vasari: See Part I. We would know next to nothing if it were not for this great, great man (even if he does scratch his boys during sex).

Viroli Maurizio, *Niccolo's Smile, A Biography of Machiavelli*, 1998

Made in United States
North Haven, CT
08 October 2022